FAR OUT

POEMS OF THE '60S

"Miss Tree" by Jim Harter

FAR OUT

POEMS OF THE '60S

EDITED BY

WENDY BARKER

'&

DAVE PARSONS

WingsPress

San Antonio, Texas

2016

Far Out: Poems of the '60s © 2016
by Wings Press
All rights revert to the individual editors, authors, and artists.

Frontispiece: "Miss Tree" © 2003 by Jim Harter.
Used by permission of the artist.

ISBN: 978-1-60940-501-4 (Paperback)

E-books:

ePub: 978-1-60940-502-1
Mobipocket/Kindle: 978-1-60940-503-8
Library PDF: 978-1-60940-504-5

Wings Press
627 E. Guenther
San Antonio, Texas 78210
Phone/fax: (210) 271-7805
On-line catalogue and ordering:
www.wingspress.com

Wings Press books are distributed to the trade by
Independent Publishers Group
www.ipgbook.com

Cataloging In Publication:

Far Out: Poems of the '60s / edited by Wendy Barker and Dave
Parsons.
        pages cm
    Includes bibliographical references.
    ISBN 978-1-60940-501-4 (paperback : alk. paper) -- ISBN 978-
1-60940-502-1 (epub ebook) -- ISBN 978-1-60940-503-8 (kindle-
mobipocket ebook) -- ISBN 978-1-60940-504-5 (library pdf
ebook)
Subjects: LCSH: American poetry--20th century. | Nineteen
sixties--Poetry. | Counterculture--United States--Poetry. | United
States--Social conditions--Poetry. | BISAC: POETRY / American
/ General.
LCC PS615 .F28 2016
811/.508--dc23
LC record available at http://lccn.loc.gov/2015047081

CONTENTS

Preface   *xiii*

I. THE PRELUDE:
what's that sound

Chana Bloch	Chez Pierre, 1961	3
Robert Alexander	A Joe Pass Guitar Solo	4
Carol Newman	Simplicity	6
Fleda Brown	Tillywilly Fog	7
Robert Phillips	To Aaron Copland	9
Rita Dove	The Enactment	10
Maxine Kumin	New Year's Eve 1959	12
Stanley Plumly	Glenn Gould	14
Andrea Potos	Birthday Parties in the '60s	15
Robert Phillips	For the Late Great	
	Pennsylvania Station	16
Rita Dove	Rosa	18
Paula Anne Yup	Waiting	19
Randall Watson	Trailways, August 28, 1963	20
W.E. Butts	Our Father's Clothes	23
Michael Waters	Dog in Space	25
Janet McCann	Chicago, 1964	26

II. DISMANTLING:
r–e–s–p–e–c–t

Alice Friman	Geometry	29
Bonnie Lyons	Mother to Daughter (1960)	31
Judy Kronenfeld	*Noblesse Oblige*	33
Lucille Lang Day	Fifteen	34
Natasha Trethewey	Self-Employment, 1970	35

Scott Wiggerman	Before the Pill	36
Lucille Lang Day	Reject Jell-O	37
Judith Arcana	Women's Liberation	38
Alice Friman	The Poet	40
Wendy Barker	*The Feminine Mystique*	43
Diane Wakoski	Love Letter Postmarked Von Beethoven	44
Diane Wakoski	Filling the Boxes of Joseph Cornell	47
George Ella Lyon	Mary	53
Robert Bonazzi	César Vallejo Died On A Rainy Night	56

III. ACCELERATION:
the times a changing

Leon Stokesbury	The Day Kennedy Died	59
Jim Daniels	Soul Sacrifice	61
David Kirby	The Summer of the Cuban Missile Crisis	63
Dede Fox	California Dreaming, LA 1966	68
Martín Espada	Public School 190, Brooklyn, 1963	70
W. E. Butts	The Industrial Diamonds of 1964	71
Bryce Milligan	Four-Stroke	73
Jim Elledge	Duckling, Swan	76
Richard Wilbur	A Miltonic Sonnet for Mr. Johnson on His Refusal of Peter Hurd's Official Portrait	78
Sandra M. Gilbert	Her Last Sickness	79
Martín Espada	The Sign in My Father's Hands	80
Fleda Brown	Where She Was, Where He Was	82
Beverly Matherne	Sons	83
Dave Parsons	Austin Fire	86
Ai	Cuba, 1962	90
Paul Mariani	Brotherhood	91

Richard Wilbur	For the Student Strikers	94
Ginny Lowe Conners	Optical Longings and Illusions	95
W. E. Butts	The Other Language	96
David Jauss	Beauty	98
Alice Friman	Dallas	100

IV. ENACTMENTS:
people get ready

C.K. Williams	King	105
Wendy Barker	Teaching *Uncle Tom's Children*	111
Alan Shapiro	Between Assassinations	112
Toi Derricotte	Blackbottom	114
Natasha Trethewey	Saturday Matinee	116
Alan Shapiro	The Fight	118
Patricia Smith	Ain't But One Way Heaven Makes Sense; Or, Annie Pearl Smith Explains the U.S. Space Program	120
Ana Castillo	Dirty Mexican	121
Patricia Smith	Asking for a Heart Attack	122
Kate Daniels	Late Apology to Doris Haskins	124
Sybil Estess	In My Alice Blue Gown	125
Rebecca Balcárcel	Ave America	128
Tim Seibles	Allison Wolff	130
Danny Romero	This Day	133
Lorenzo Thomas	Back in the Day	134

V. WAR PHOTOGRAPHS:
there's a man with a gun over there

Robert Bly	At a March Against the Vietnam War	139
Chana Bloch	The Spoils	140
Kate Daniels	War Photograph	141
Tess Gallagher	Sugarcane	143

H. Palmer Hall	This Poem	146
H. Palmer Hall	We Have Seen the Enemy	147
H. Palmer Hall	Father Buddha	148
Judith Arcana	Correspondence	149
Edward Hirsch	The Lottery	151
David Huddle	Nerves	152
David Huddle	Them	154
David Huddle	Work	155
David Jauss	The Border	156
Michael Anania	A Second-Hand Elegy	158
Yusef Komunyakaa	Communique	160
Yusef Komunyakaa	Tu Do Sheet	162
Yusef Komunyakaa	Hanoi Hannah	164
Alicia Ostriker	VOX POPULI	166
Stanley Plumly	The Day of the Failure in Saigon, Thousands in the Streets, Hundreds Killed, a Lucky Few Hanging On the Runners of Evacuating Copters	167
Patricia Smith	Minus One, Minus One More	169
Katherine Solomon	Expatriates, 1967	170
Alicia Ostriker	Cambodia	173

VI. SEX (EDUCATION):
baby, light my fire

Sally Lipton Derringer	After the Gold Rush	181
Alberto Ríos	Like This It Is We Think To Dance	183
Susan Firer	Saint Valentine's Day, 1967	184
Tim Seibles	Delores Jepps	187
Tim Seibles	Terry Moore	190
Andrea Potos	To Want the Man	193
Kent Newkirk	Sex Education	195
Martha Serpas	In Praise of the Passion Mark	197
Richard Wilbur	Playboy	199
Paul Ruffin	Billly's Rubbers	201

VII. DRUGS AND ROCK 'N' ROLL:
dance beneath the diamond sky

Alan Shapiro	Mud Dancing	205
Bryce Milligan	Song for a Highway Angel	207
Lorna Dee Cervantes	Cream	209
Vivian Shipley	Charlie's Asleep at the Wire Waiting for You to Sleep	210
Aliki Barnstone	In the Workshop	212
Dave Parsons	Austin Relativity	214
Alicia Ostriker	Satisfaction	216
Kent Newkirk	Tripping Through Life, Fantastic!	218
Dave Parsons	Night Hawk	220
Edward Hirsch	Days of 1968	221
Tim Hunt	Ravi Shankar After the Show	222
Lucille Lang Day	The Trip	223
Katherine Solomon	A Momentarily Subdued Foofaraw	224
Barbara Hamby	Ode to Rock 'n' Roll	227
Vivian Shipley	Hike Up Av. Du Pere-Lachaise	229
Michael Waters	Christ at the Apollo, 1962	230
Jim Elledge	Strangers: An Essay	232
Adrian C. Louis	Listening to the Doors	235
Jim Daniels	Jimi Hendrix, National Anthem	236
Edward Hirsch	The Burning of the Midnight Lamp	237

VIII. AFTERMATH
the answer, blowing in the wind

Hunt Hawkins	The Revolution in Oakland	243
Ted Kooser	Shame	245
Vivian Shipley	Obeying Glands	247
Judith Arcana	The Sun in Montana	249
Ginny Lowe Connors	Reunion	250
Leon Stokesbury	Evening's End: 1943-1970	253
Kathleen Winter	Nostalgia for Apollo	259

Kate Daniels	Homage to Calvin Spotswood	260
Paul Mariani	The Things They Taught Me	265
Kevin Clark	Eight Hours in the Nixon Era	269
Peter Balakian	Reading Dickinson/Summer '68	273
Adrian C. Louis	San Francisco: 1969	275
C.K. Williams	The Poet	277
Adrian C. Louis	April 24, 1971	282
Robert Phillips	The Death of Janis Joplin	283
Janet Lowery	The *Dharma Kia* Foundation	285
Jim Daniels	Shedding the Sixties	288
Stephen Dunn	The Sexual Revolution	289
David Lehman	Paris, 1971	291
Stanley Plumly	Four Hundred Mourners	295
Stephen Dunn	Around the Time of the Moon	297
Jim Elledge	"Their Hats is Always White"	298
Michael Waters	Sixties Sonnet	300
Martín Espada	The Year I Was Diagnosed With a Sacrilegious Heart	301
Janet McCann	In Front of the Coke Machine	303
Wendy Barker	Miniskirts	304
Robert Bly	Driving West in 1970	305
About the Poets		307
Acknowledgments		357

*For all the veterans:
from Selma to Vietnam to Kent State,
from Columbia to San Francisco State,
Greenwich Village to Haight-Ashbury ...*

PREFACE

Who first said "If you remember the '60s you weren't there"? Was it Grace Slick (according to Jerry Hopkins in *Bangkok Babylon*, 2006)? Or Paul Kantner (in *The New Yorker* in 1991)? Or Judy Collins, George Harrison, or even Robin Williams? But whoever is responsible for this flip, all-too-glib statement with its sly drug-related allusion could not have read the dazzling range of poems we've included here in *Far Out: Poems of the '60s*.

In December 2009, driving to Houston's Hobby Airport for Wendy's flight back to San Antonio after she'd given a reading at Montgomery College, where Dave teaches, we conceived the plan for compiling this collection. Each of us had recently published poems dealing with our experiences during the explosive decade of the '60s—Dave's collection, *Color of Mourning* (Texas Review Press), included a hefty section of poems about his years serving in the U.S. Marine Corps and then working his way through college in Austin; and Wendy's "novel" in prose poems, *Nothing Between Us: The Berkeley Years* (Del Sol Press), traced interracial experiences while teaching ninth-grade English in West Berkeley, a few blocks from the newly formed Black Panthers headquarters.

During the drive, Dave observed that whenever he read poems from his book about coming of age in Austin during the '60s, listeners rushed up to him after the reading to give thanks for bringing a particular memory to mind or to relate their own experiences. Eyes on the road, hands on the wheel of his Nissan Xterra, Dave casually mentioned to Wendy that he'd been thinking about doing an anthology of Austin '60s poems. Wendy said that she had also been receiving similar enthusiastic reactions to her '60s poems, and not only from people old enough to remember those years. Then she burst out, "Hey, what if we co-edited a collection of poems by poets nationwide about the '60s?" And *Far Out: Poems of the '60s* was born.

Dave shared the fact that he had been profoundly moved by William Jay Smith's much-lauded *Cherokee Lottery*, which includes poems in the voices of Indians, soldiers, bystanders, and politicians during the Trail of Tears, the forced removal from their homelands of the Cherokee, Muscogee, Seminole, Chickasaw, and Choctaw Nations. What better way, Dave continued, to relate historical events than through vividly realized poems? Of course, we are in no way comparing the realities of most lives in the U.S. during the 1960s to the displacement of tens of thousands during the horrendous, shameful Trail of Tears. Naturally our focus would be entirely different, incorporating poems written from the point of view of those who were alive in the '60s, writing of their own distinctive experiences.

And as we began to discuss our goals for the book, we immediately agreed that we were interested in poems that expressed specific personal histories or reflections on the period between 1958 or 1959 and 1971 or 1972—from the years leading up to the ones we associate most with the '60s to the years immediately following. We also knew from the outset we did not want to include poems simply railing in general terms about ideology, the war, drugs, feminism, music, or civil rights. And this would not be a book of poetry written during the '60s, but mainly of poetry looking back—of, oh yes, of people actually remembering the '60s!

Of course, we've made a couple of exceptions (to prove the rule?). We couldn't omit, for instance, Diane Wakoski's furious, iconic early feminist poems "Filling the Boxes of Joseph Cornell" from *Inside the Blood Factory* (1968) or "Love Letter Postmarked Von Beethoven" from *The Motorcycle Betrayal Poems* (1972). We also believed it essential to include two of Rita Dove's elegant, powerful poems from *On the Bus With Rosa Parks* (W. W. Norton & Company, 1999), even though it was in 1955 that Rosa Parks was arrested for refusing to give up her seat in the white section of a Montgomery, Alabama bus. But since historians call that incident the birth of the American Civil Rights Movement, which burgeoned during the '60s, we simply couldn't omit "Rosa" and "The Enactment."

But why a book about the decade of the '60s? Why not the '50s, or the '70s? And why divide time by decades at all? Every era strikes us as having its own particular zeitgeist, though some periods affect us afterward more than others, which, we would argue, is the case with the '60s. The assassinations of Medgar Evers (1963), John F. Kennedy (1963), Malcolm X (1965), Martin Luther King (1968), and Robert Kennedy (1968) sent shock waves into all corners of the United States. Many have argued that the assassination of JFK signaled the end of innocence in our country. In 1966, on the University of Texas campus in Austin, Charles Whitman shot forty-three people, killing thirteen of them in a massacre that introduced our country to the idea of mass murder in a public space and spurred the creation of SWAT teams across the nation.

The U.S. military involvement in Vietnam, at the outset viewed as necessary to prevent a Communist take-over of South Vietnam, increased during the '60s, with troop levels tripling in 1961 and 1962 and rising even further in 1964 and 1965. After the death of JFK and the Gulf of Tonkin incident of 1964, opposition to the war escalated. The growing resistance, especially among the young, pitted generations, even family members, against each other, and ultimately resulted in an end to the draft and the conversion of our country's military into an all-volunteer force.

Student protests across the country at the University of California at Berkeley, Jackson State University, Columbia University, and Kent State University led to massive violence. During the '60s, those under thirty—who for the first time in U.S. history outnumbered their elders—were challenging older folks in unprecedented ways, as the youthful counterculture became a significant, volatile force. Beyond our own borders, social turmoil, often accompanied by violence and even massacres, occurred in France, Mexico, Brazil, Poland, Spain, China, Germany, and Czechoslovakia.

Other hierarchies in our nation were shaken up by the rise of Second-Wave Feminism and the Civil Rights Movement. In 1963, Betty Friedan's bestselling *The Feminine Mystique* was published and the Equal Pay Act was passed. NOW (the National Organization for Women) was formed in 1966. FDA approval of the Pill in 1960 led to 12.5 million women using oral contraceptives by 1967. Martin Luther King gave his "I Have a Dream" speech before hundreds of thousands in Washington, D.C. in 1963; the Civil Rights Act of 1964 authorized federal action against segregation in public accommodations, public facilities, and employment; the Voting Rights Act of 1965 was passed after large demonstrations in Selma, Alabama; and the Fair Housing Act, prohibiting discrimination by race in housing, was passed in 1968, by which time many Black radicals were pushing not for peaceful integration, but for Black Power.

The Chicano Movement, a continuation of the 1940s Mexican American Civil Rights Movement, was inspired not only by the African-American Civil Rights Movement but also by the Young Lords, a Puerto Rican nationalist group. *El movimiento* brought about numerous changes in education, politics, the criminal justice system, art, the church, health, employment, and housing—and gave birth to Chicano literature. The United Farm Workers Organizing Committee, formed in 1962 by Cesar Chavez, Dolores Huerta, and Philip Vera Cruz, used non-violent tactics such as boycotts, marches, and strikes to improve working conditions. The organization's name was changed to the United Farm Workers Union in 1972. Rodolfo "Corky" Gonzáles' poem "Yo Soy Joaquin" helped define the meaning of being a Chicano; the epic poem was adapted into a film in 1969 by Luis Valdez, who himself had founded El Teatro Campesino. In 1968, the Mexican American Legal Defense and Educational Fund (MALDEF) was founded.

Also inspired by the African-American Civil Rights movement were Native Americans. In 1964, a group of Sioux occupied San Francisco Bay's Alcatraz Island for four hours; between 1969 and 1971, as many as four hundred Native Americans from numerous tribes occupied the island, which brought international attention to the situation of indigenous peoples in the U.S. and set a precedent for Indian activism, as well as leading to the passage of the Indian Self-Determination and Education Assistance Act of 1975. The American Indian Movement (AIM) was founded in Minneapolis in 1968, and worked closely with the Rainbow Coalition to protest human rights violations.

The Stonewall riots of 1969—prompted by undercover police harassment and suppressed by the New York City Police "riot squad"—led to large demonstrations by gays and lesbians in Greenwich Village, and eventually to the first Gay Pride marches, the founding of gay rights organizations, and the work toward establishing LGBT rights in the United States.

Previously held boundaries of all sorts were dissolved, including the one between Earth and "the heavens." In 1961 President Kennedy proclaimed before Congress his goal of landing a man on the moon within the decade. In 1962, John Glenn was the first American to orbit Earth; in 1969, Neil Armstrong of the Apollo 11 crew walked on the moon. And back on Earth, the modern environmental movement began in the '60s— Rachel Carson's *Silent Spring* was published in 1962, the Clean Air Act was passed in 1963, the first *Whole Earth Catalog* appeared in 1968, and Friends of the Earth was founded in 1969.

All these changes were mind-blowing, to use the lingo of the times. No wonder Bob Dylan's song from 1964 might be the best anthem of all for this period, for the times were radically "a changin'." As Morris Dickstein puts it in his *Gates Of Eden: American Culture in the Sixties* (W. W. Norton & Company, 1977), during these years "the moral lives of Americans went through a sea change."

Not surprisingly, popular music expresses much of the '60s' zeitgeist. Identification with particular musical groups or singers can also say much about where a person was—or who that person was—during the '60s. When the two of us, for instance, began listing memorable lyrics in an attempt to provide subtitles for the separate sections of this anthology, how our choices differed! Dave was all Bob Dylan, Buddy Holly, and The Rolling Stones; Wendy: Ray Charles, Aretha Franklin, the Mamas and the Papas. Though of course we merged on the Beatles, on Joan Baez, Peter, Paul and Mary, Simon and Garfunkel, and The New Christy Minstrels. But a list of the era's most beloved musicians and musical groups could go on forever, including Janis Joplin, The Supremes, Miles Davis, Pete Seeger, Dionne Warwick, Carlos Santana, Linda Ronstadt, Marvin Gaye, Blood, Sweat, and Tears, and anything out of Motown.

Obviously, this is not the place to list all the music, the cultural and political struggles and events, all the happenings from the '60s—if we did, there would be no room for the richly varied poems included here. When we put out our invitations for poets to submit work for our collection, we were not prepared for the avalanche of poems we received, from writers who were born long before the Baby Boom—the population explosion that began after WWII in the mid-1940s—and even from writers who were still children in the '60s. But of course, the majority of our contributors were in their teens or twenties during the decade. We only wish we could have included more of the many fine poems offered to us!

We extend our gratitude to Sonya Barrera Eddy, whose organizational help at the initial stages of our project made it possible for us to continue. And without the efficient, superb assistance of Stephanie Schoellman throughout, the book would never have been born. We cannot thank her enough. We are grateful to Bryce Milligan of Wings Press for his enthusiastic, dedicated commitment. We are also grateful to our spouses for their support, to Wendy's husband Steven G. Kellman for assiduous fact-checking and copy-editing and to Dave's wife Nancy Parsons for her reliable memory and artist's eye. And, of course, we owe gigantic thanks to all the writers whose poems contribute to the multi-textured strands that comprise *Far Out: Poems of the '60s,* which we hope serves to portray the rich weave, the variegated textures of this kaleidoscopic era. "Those

Were the Days, My Friend," sang the Limelighters in the early 1960s and Mary Hopkin a bit later, in 1968. May this collection vividly recall—and validate—the days of this decade for those who lived through them and bring them to life for those too young to have been there with us.

—Wendy Barker and Dave Parsons

I.

THE PRELUDE

what's that sound

Chana Bloch

Chez Pierre, 1961

The skirt's all wrong and the shoes
pinch: thin straps
and little pointed heels. Borrowed clothing.
She crosses her legs under the table.
Uncrosses them.

Heat rises heavy, a raincloud
gathering moisture.
His hand comes down over hers.
Look at those couples: their lives
are already a downpour.

She can't imagine me yet
though she's starting that puzzled
tuck around the mouth,
the one I'm just getting used to.
He draws little *O*s on her palm

with a fingernail, laughing, taking
his time. I still
carry her with me, unfinished,
into the hazard
of other people's hands,

I live with her choices.
The waiter says, *Sweet
or dry?* and wipes the dew from a bottle.
She's got to decide, tonight!
for my life to begin.

Robert Alexander

A Joe Pass Guitar Solo

I've fallen asleep in the afternoon. It's November and the radio is playing a jazz program from the local Public Radio station. But my father and I are in Fenway Park. It's June and the outfield grass is dark green (darker than the huge green left-field wall) and my father has just bought one of those ten-cent paper bags of peanuts (it must be close to a full pound of peanuts for a dime). We're both eating peanuts. My father's hands—which seem huge to me, the backs covered with veins "like a roadmap" as he used to say—are deft as hell with the peanuts: Crack and he tosses them into his mouth, the shells drop through the green slats of the seat.

It's the eighth inning and the Red Sox are behind by five runs. Ted Williams is batting and my father points out to me how perfect his swing is. "Look at that bastard swing," my father says—"level as Nebraska." I don't think my father was ever in Nebraska. "But remember, Rob," he says, "he only hit .400 in his really good years. . . . Even at his best Ted Williams missed the ball six times out of ten."

It's getting to the end of my dream. I'm in that funny place where you're dreaming but you're also aware of the room around you. There's late-afternoon sunlight through the plants in my window and it sounds like Joe Pass on the radio, bass and piano comping in the background. Joe Pass's left hand is going all over the fingerboard of his arch-top Gibson and his right hand is in perfect time. The notes are like tropical birds flying from the small speaker of my radio . . . and suddenly all these

bright yellow and blue and orange birds come circling
and wheeling into Fenway Park. My father and I look up
amazed at the bird-filled June sky.

Carol Newman

Simplicity

The window over the sink
looks out past the clothesline
where Sherry's mother hangs dishtowels,
her *Bunny Bread* tee shirt, and her father's
work pants. 'KB' radio bounces off the refrigerator.
It is 1959. We are dancing

in the kitchen. This is before
we watch *I Love Lucy,* spill grape juice
on the rug, after we made *Cocoa Surprise Cookies.*
Sherry rinses glasses, shimmies to the drying
rack. I dry, sashay past the double-oven Tappan,
twirl along the table's chrome edges, careful

of the glass swan where they drop their keys.
This is after Miss Schwabenbauer's red fingernails
traced ovaries, uterus, fallopian tubes, before
we knew what she meant by *menopause
means you're old.* Our socks glide
on clean yellow linoleum, dust-mopped

smooth. Outside, in rows like spectators,
red-winged blackbirds watch cows ruminate
on Jordan's Hill; telephone wires hum
under their feet. It is morning. Ahead of us,
the day stretches out as far as we can see.
It is 1959. We are dancing in the kitchen.

Fleda Brown

Tillywilly Fog

I'm kissing his poster, on my knees on my bed.
We're both children, in a way. Maybe we stop
at fifteen. We could easily be in the fogged-
up car at Tillywilly Quarry. We haven't, you know,
yet. It begins here. The rest seems like a vast
openness. I cannot imagine past his hand

up my skirt any more than he could imagine handing
back his songs to silence, or lying on his death-bed
without Priscilla or Kathy or Linda or Jo or vast
numbers of other girls called in to stop
his mind enough so he could sleep. What we know
together is half-shut eyes, call it a fog

of desire, if you want, but there is something in the fog
that is not us, an alertness of mind, a hand
running over the entirety of what we know
and calling it good. No matter whose bed
you get in later, something in your mind stops
here: you and Elvis touch lips across the vast

distance. *Don't* sap this up: the truth is vaster
than the jewel-belted icon stumbling in a fog
of barbiturates. The vibration of the universe never stops.
It's all song, the hum of molecules in the hand
and lips, and what goes away comes back, a flower-bed
of humming, spilling over the edge of what you know.

You think the fat women who cried didn't know
what they cried for, when he died? It's no vast
distance between them and me. Our souls are bedded
in our hungry bodies, taking advantage of the fog
at Tillywilly. "Please let me put my hand
there," he says, and being scared, he stops

there. Nothing ever felt this good, to stop
on that note, the mouth wide open, no
thought left, no design, waiting for the hand
of God to move on or intervene. It's vastness,
it's plenty, it's human spring, pure song, a fog
of wastefulness. You get out of bed

the rest of your life knowing it's Elvis's bed
you've come from–vast, vibrating. On the one hand,
you're stopped, flesh and bone; on the other, you're a song.

Robert Phillips

To Aaron Copland

On His Sixtieth Birthday. 1960.

Suffused light focused into brilliance of blazing
          poppies
Sprung forth full grown from sparse Appalachian
          soil:
You have given us adagios and allegros of feeling
          that soar
Over grazed grasses and glazed glasses of a nation
Balloon-bursting with joy and hysteria.
                    Shaker, Quaker, farmhand, bigcity Jew—
All are here—sprightly, rightly denim dancing to
          the groan
And thwack of tractors and threshing machines.
Brazen henna-haired Jazz descends upon a New
          England town,
Assaulting the immaculate and austere moods of
          sunparlors
And hundreds of stingily-lit, yam-filled sewing
          rooms.
                    Ascend your podium, Maestro-Composer!
Give the tender land more—more ripe rhythms,
          plump
Music to pleasure a tinseled, troubled day.

Rita Dove

The Enactment

*"I'm just a girl who people were mean to
on a bus. . .I could have been anybody."*
—Mary Ware, Née Smith

Can't use no teenager, especially
no poor black trash,
no matter what her parents do
to keep up a living. Can't use
anyone without sense enough
to bite their tongue.

It's gotta be a woman,
someone of standing:
preferably shy, preferably married.
And she's got to know
when the moment's right.
Stay polite, though her shoulder's
aching, bus driver
the same one threw her off
twelve years before.

Then all she's got to do is
sit there, quiet, till
the next moment finds her—and only then
can she open her mouth to ask
Why do you push us around?
and his answer: *I don't know but
the law is the law and you*

are under arrest.
She must sit there, and not smile
as they enter to carry her off;
she must know who to call
who will know whom else to call
to bail her out. . . and only then

can she stand up and exhale,
can she walk out the cell
and down the jail steps
into flashbulbs and
her employer's white
arms—and go home,
and sit down in the seat
we have prepared for her.

Maxine Kumin

New Year's Eve 1959

remembering Anne Sexton and Jack Geiger

This was the way we used to party:
lamps unplugged, shoved in the closet
rugs rolled up, furniture pushed back
Glenn Miller singles on the spindle.

There was the poet kicking off her shoes
to jitterbug with the Physician
for Social Responsibility
the only time they ever met

and he pecking his head to the beat
swinging her out on the stalk of his arm
setting all eight gores of her skirt
twirling, then hauling her in for a Fred

Astaire session of deep dips
and both of them cutting out to strut
humming along with the riffs
that punctuated "Chattanooga Choo Choo."

This was after Seoul and before Saigon.
Coke was still a carbonated drink
we added rum to. There was French wine
but someone had misplaced the curlicue

and a not-yet famous novelist
magicked the cork out on the hinge
of the back door to "Sunrise Serenade"
and dance was the dark enabler.

Lights off a long minute at midnight
(squeals and false moans) madcap Anne
long dead now and Jack snowily
balding who led the drive to halt the bomb

and I alone am saved to tell you
how they could jive.

Stanley Plumly

Glenn Gould

I heard him that one night in Cincinnati.
The concert hall, 1960, the same day
Kennedy flew into town in perfect sunlight
and rode the route that took him
through the crowds of voters and nonvoters
who alike seemed to want to climb
into the armored convertible.
Gould did not so much play as address
the piano from a height of inches,
as if he were trying to slow the music
by holding each note separately.
Later he would say he was tired
of making public appearances,
the repetition of performing the Variations
was killing him. But that night
Bach felt like a discovery, whose repetitions
Gould had practiced in such privacy
as to bring them into being for the first time.
This was the fall, October, when Ohio,
like almost every other part of the country,
is beginning to be mortally beautiful,
the great old hardwoods letting go
their various scarlet, yellow,
and leopard-spotted leaves one by one.

Andrea Potos

Birthday Parties in the '60s

These were the parties of living rooms
with shag rugs and velour armchairs,
hairsprayed mothers hovering with Polaroids,
and handfuls of girls with bandana blindfolds,
attaching the tail to the donkey's legs, nose, bottom;

the grueling, delicious trial
of the spanking mill—the birthday girl with no choice
but to crawl through the tunnel
of ferocious girls, to be sprung

from between their legs splayed apart
as if rehearsing for events twenty years to come,
all of them, emerging flushed and ravenous,

aiming for the linen clad table,
the reign of the tall round cake
smothered in a sculpture of pink roses.

Robert Phillips

For the Late Great Pennsylvania Station

(1910 – 1966)

"What is our praise or pride but to imagine
Excellence and try to make it?" the poet asked.
Man made it in Manhattan, a dream of pure glory,
        Ornamented by the eagles of Caesars,
        Walled in creamy gold travertine.

Vaunting Doric columns supported a vaulting
Crystal ceiling one-hundred-fifty feet high,
Waiting room the length of two city blocks,
        Space suitable for history to stretch out legs in.
        Exposed structural steel counterpointed,

Spoke to us of the Modern Age's motion and power,
Sepia murals whispered like Penn's Woods' past.
This was our immense New World temple.
        This was our expansiveness and light,
        Interior vista vast as our continent.

When you arrived there, you knew you knew
You had arrived. It cast long shadows,
Contained the sounds of time, for merely
        Fifty-six years—not even a blink.
        Then it fell to greed,

To demolishers of glory, for a chrome
And plastic sports dome that could have squatted
Anywhere. I recollected Ilion and Babylon,
       Coventry and Dresden—hymns to joy, alas.
       That which man has made, *homo perdidit.*

Rita Dove

Rosa

How she sat there,
the time right inside a place
so wrong it was ready.

That trim name with
its dream of a bench
to rest on. Her sensible coat.

Doing nothing was the doing:
the clean flame of her gaze
carved by a camera flash.

How she stood up
when they bent down to retrieve
her purse. That courtesy.

Paula Anne Yup

Waiting

My sister remembers how we lived
five children in a small house
horrible the lack of money
and a doll in a wedding dress for us two to share
so beautiful in the package she remembers
how lovely, lovely wanting to touch
but we didn't have permission from our parents.
For the doll to last
it had to stay in the package and we could only look
at the white dress and the doll in a box.

My sister remembers the longing
to touch the loveliness and to play
little child only wanting to hold and hold
to hug and hug and dress and undress
like a little girl should so it became too much
she pocked a hole through the plastic
so she could touch but it wasn't nearly enough
she says all these years later: not enough at all

Randall Watson

Trailways, August 28, 1963

We crossed the exhilarating, high-pitched.
Passed the stench and glittering,
the amusement bright, the gradual,
box apartments by the tracks and stations
squatting like bored and patient orphans
waiting for a Sunday market to begin.

Then the green-bordered interstates.

Hay bales scattered like formalist sculptures, cornfields
with their stiff stalks and rag-doll tassels
limp as puppets hung
in a storage closet.
Side woods snarled with briar and ivy.
Oaks and maples.

Then Rummy and Old Maid
at the little table rearward and nearby
the cramped bathrooms
that stank of chemicals and soap and piss
splattered on the metal floor, flecks
of snow-white shaving foam
clinging to the shadowy mirror.

Racks of bags and suitcases and light jackets
dreaming above our heads
like hibernating mammals.

The chrome bright
burnings of the little towns,

those signs for Burma Shave and Stuckey's and
The World's Largest Rabbit
and men in large hats and fringed buckskin
wearing side arms on the porch
of a mock saloon.

Birds scrolling the staves of the infrastructure.

Men outside a church
brushing ashes from their sleeves.

Wives and daughters and mothers touching their hair
as if to measure themselves,

waving little paper fans
stapled to paint sticks
where Jesus kneels, alone
in the midst of his drowsy, sleeping disciples,
knowing the story his body will tell.

And then my grandfather
sitting on the back stoop with his .22
shooting sparrows, which dirty the sidewalk.

Dust blowing off the fields.

Small purple flowers
speckled with dew and foraging ants.

He's dipping bread in a cup of milk, disregarding
the plate of tomatoes, red as transitions.

Crushing his Pall Mall in the drive.

Pulling two hot 7 Ups from the trunk
of his Oldsmobile.

And those boys
in jeans jackets who gather
outside Peguy's,
the only women's clothing store in town,
car hoods raised, adjusting
the air intake or idle, gunning
the engine.

Wiping the oil stick clean
with a slash of newsprint.

Attuned to the mechanical contrivance.

Discovering their blurred faces in the polished armature.

There near the geographical
heart of the country.

38 North by 97 West.

Entranced by the sheen.

W. E. Butts

Our Fathers' Clothes

And so now we wanted other lives,
sixteen years old on a summer evening,
coming out of the small town's theater
after "Dr. No"—Ursula Andress in a bikini,
suddenly emerging on a white Jamaican beach,
suntanned and rapt with private song;
Connery as Bond, dark browed and sexual,
stepping out from behind a dune, singing back.
And later, in a perfect tuxedo, Bond wins
at roulette, and deftly places a chip
in the cleavage of that night's good fortune.
These were not our fathers' clothes—
those men of field and factory labor,
Friday's poker ante, Schaefer beer,
a cigar's reward, gabardine trousers,
and rolled up sleeves. But when we stopped
at the Hickey-Freeman men's store
window, our reflected images
dissolved the manikins' blank stares,
until we boys became the characters
in a movie of our own making, confident as men
dressed in slightly tilted fedoras, carefully peaked
handkerchiefs pointing out the breast pockets
of our blended wool, three-button coats,
jacquard print ties in Windsor knots
on Hathaway shirts, the cuffs of pleated pants
just breaking over polished oxfords.
Then a fade to the final scene:

we walked home through the dimly-lit streets—
our fathers' sons.

Michael Waters

Dog in Space

Friday nights on WINS
Murray the K counted down the Top Ten.
A boy who loved the idea of order—
All objects having their place in the world—
I recorded each hit, its spot on the chart,
Then rummaged for meaning in weekly lists
As solemn scholars combed Dead Sea Scrolls.
The names of songs seemed *almost* Biblical—
My rapt concentration a kind of prayer,
Though only a Russian dog gazed down.
Tin Pan Alley was my chapel as cheap
Transistors spewed revival. Ecstatic
Cries suffused Brooklyn wilderness.
The lists warned how sinners would be ranked,
Culled from mausoleums come Judgment Day.
I Will Follow Him. It's Now or Never.
Like a smash hit played each hour all summer,
The canine cosmonaut spun overhead.
If I searched hard when the countdown ended,
I could spot the spark of the satellite
Among mute stars, crossing the sky, then hear
The weak, unanswered bark.

Janet McCann

Chicago, 1964

We picked the seminarians up behind
Archbishop Quigley's, they wore
their black habits to cross the yard
unobserved, climbed over the wall

to the waiting car. What a party
it would be, we would drink and talk
God all night and eat the pasta
we all lived on, vegetarian, but

meatballs kept separate for the
less enlightened ones. One night
the woman who read palms
told us all our marriages

and late or early deaths, and she
said two of three seminarians
had no marriage crosses, though the third
did and he would be no priest.

Someone told me later he had quit
the seminary. All I remember is
looking into the palm of one of the
chosen two, the head line, the

heart line, and a smooth patch between—
slightly plump, unmarked and virginal.

II.

DISMANTLING

r-e-s-p-e-c-t

Alice Friman

Geometry

Mono-buttocked in a girdle,
& brassiered into cones—their satin
sister act pointy under wraps—we were
more than Euclidian globes & conicals
or the buzzy triangle we struggled
not to think about. If we were
two-faced & all angles toward
matrimony as we were accused,
let me assure you, we were obtuse.
To us, men were problems to be
solved & corrected, not the answers
at the back of the book.
                              And how we
loved our books, clutched them
to our cardigans: Keats, Tolstoy,
Thomas Wolfe, Dostoevsky, anyone
with compass or T-square enough
to take the full measure of what
we were: Faust, not Gretchen. Socrates
defining wisdom in the marketplace
not Xanthippe at home pounding out
the phyllo for the baklava. We were told
The Trojan Women was man, his suffering,
& we swallowed it, for didn't we too
switch genders for sense & sanity,
laying claim to Ahab's search for truth
in a book of seas, or the phantom itself
hurtling beyond definition?

                                      Of those
who held up the mirror showing us
a jumble of geometry, laying us out
in garish polygons & tortured trapezoids—
we argued the merits of modem art,
turned away & paid the price.
                                      We wore
our hair-shirts starched & suffered
our virtue gladly. In short, we were afraid.
In love with love, we strained
at the forbidden line. If coerced,
cajoled, or back-seat outmaneuvered,
the next day brought roses, brought *Sorry,
it won't happen again.*
                                 Was it to our credit,
agreeing to believe the unbelievable?
Were we right to take the high road,
to play the game we couldn't win?
The satin was cut & measured before
we filled our cups, & the only formula
to solve for was the axiom behind the veil:
complement, make the incongruous,
congruous. The threatening acute, right.

Bonnie Lyons

Mother to Daughter (1960)

Prepare your fortress.
Our ancestors knew
not to let fingernail clippings
or hair fall
into the wrong hands.
And we know there must be
nothing as obvious
as cigarette ashes, book, or cushion
imperfectly placed.
No signs of untidy life
in house beautiful.

Now your armor:
First the concealed weapons.
Girdle and longline bra
and you're girded loin to chest.
Next, the crisp, coordinated outfit
with matching shoes and handbag.
Under your helmet of lacquered hair
put on your face.
Base, powder, lipstick, mascara.
Now you're ready.

Mr. Rejection and his big brother
Mr. Death (maybe I shouldn't
mention his name)
can peek in the window
but they won't dare dare dare
knock on your door.

All you have to do now
is not move.

You're sitting pretty.

Judy Kronenfeld

Noblesse Oblige

She was well-married as Miranda
to Ferdinand, zippy as Rosalind
in Arden, pony-tailed like a kid,
at her first MLA in 1971, when the handsome
professor of Middle English lit
who'd taken to saying in class,
Feel free to call me Rick! (was he
newly entering the late '60s zeitgeist?) invited her
to his room on some job-search
pretext. Assuming concern
tantamount to her own
ambitions, she went, not overly
suspicious, and watched while he,
obvious as an undergraduate
cribber, poured more Scotch
than she might drink in a month
of grad-student dinners. But his lips when he
kissed her descended softly
as dewe in Aprille
that falleth on the flowr—their pressure
subtle as the most deft irony.
She helplessly savored
their touch, then begged off,
murmuring something earnest
about loyalty. He asked *Are you*
sure? then let her go,
then said—as her heart fell through all
the stories of herself like an elevator
out of control—*I'll* still *write you*
a good letter for that job.

Lucille Lang Day

Fifteen

I was pregnant that year,
stitching lace and purple-flowered ribbon
to tiny kimonos and sacques.
I still thought sperm
came out like pollen dust in puffs of air.

I ate Cream of Wheat for breakfast, unsalted,
diapered a rubber doll
in my Red Cross baby care class, and sold
lipsticks and gummy lotions to housewives
to pay for a crib.

Oh, it was something, giving birth.
When my water bag splattered
I screamed, and the neat green anesthesiologist
said, "Why don't you shut up?"
"Fuck you!" I shrieked.

"Breathe deep," was the last thing
l heard him say.
Ten minutes later I woke up.
The obstetrician with his needle and thread,
busy as a seamstress,

winked at the pink-haired nurse
who brought me my baby girl,
wrinkled and howling.
"She's lovely. I'd like a cheeseburger
and milkshake now," I said.

Natasha Trethewey

Self-Employment, 1970

Who to be today? So many choices,
all that natural human hair piled high,
curled and flipped—style after style
perched, each on its Styrofoam head.
Maybe an upsweep, or finger waves
with a ponytail. Not a day passes
that she goes unkempt—
Never know who might stop by—
now that she works at home
pacing the cutting table,
or pumping the stiff pedal
of the bought-on-time Singer.

Most days, she dresses for the weather,
relentless sun, white heat. The one tree
nearest her workroom, a mimosa,
its whimsy of pink puffs cut back
for a child's swing set. And now, grandchildren—
it's come to this—a frenzy of shouts,
the constant *slap* of an old screen door.
At least the radio still swings jazz
just above the noise, and

Ah yes, the window unit—leaky at best.
Sometimes she just stands still, lets
ice water drip onto upturned wrists.
Up under that wig, her head
sweating, hot as an idea.

Scott Wiggerman

Before the Pill

You, with a mixing bowl and apron
in your kitchen of teal and linoleum;

you, in heels, cranking the hand beater
as if an electronic mixer had never existed.

I have slammed the screen door again.
My sneakers squeak as I rush to the counter.

You, looking over your cat-eyed glasses
as my fingers reach for the bowl,

"Wash your hands first, dear,
and then you can lick the bowl."

You, with your bouffant bangs
and Elizabeth Arden lips and nails.

But this is all a dream, isn't it?
You, yellow, in an undulating aura

of cigarette smoke and cocktails.
John Lennon figured it out:

Mother, you had me,
but I never had you.

Lucille Lang Day

Reject Jell-O

The man I married twice—
at fourteen in Reno, again in Oakland
the month before I turned eighteen—
had a night maintenance job at General Foods.
He mopped the tiled floors and scrubbed
the wheels and teeth of the Jell-O machines.
I see him bending in green light,
a rag in one hand,
a pail of foamy solution at his feet.
He would come home at seven a.m.
with a box of damaged Jell-O packages,
including the day's first run,
routinely rejected, and go to sleep.
I made salad with that reject Jell-O—
lemon, lime, strawberry, orange, peach—
in a kitchen where I could almost touch
opposing walls at the same time
and kept a pie pan under the leaking sink.
We ate hamburgers and Jell-O
almost every night
and when the baby went to sleep,
we loved, snug in the darkness pierced
by passing headlights and a streetlamp's gleam,
listening to the Drifters and the Platters.
Their songs wrapped around me
like coats of fur, I hummed in the long shadows
while the man I married twice
dressed and left for work.

Judith Arcana

Women's Liberation

Every week we went to a meeting.
but not like now. No one stood up
and said, My name is Jane and I'm
an abortionist. No. Because we didn't
want to stop, we weren't trying not to do it.
We sat in apartments, passing the cards.

One card is Sandy from West Lafayette,
eighteen years old, coming in on the bus.
She's got about sixty-three dollars, she thinks
she's nine weeks pregnant. The next card is
Terrelle, who's thirty-two and angry. Her
doctor gave her an IUD that didn't work;
he says there's nothing he can do.
Here's Mona, fifty-four years old, has one
hundred dollars, wants to keep this secret
from her family. And Carlie, a long term—
twenty weeks pregnant, may have ten dollars,
twelve years old like Mona's youngest—she
got herpes from her brother when he did it.

Every week some of the cards were passed
around for hours; none of us wanted
to counsel those women, take one
into her life. The longest of long terms,
they lived far away, had no one but us,
no one to tell, no one to help, no money.
They needed everything. Cards went around

the room while we talked: dilation, syringes,
xylocaine, the Saturday list. At the end
of the meeting, all the cards were taken.

Alice Friman

The Poet

He was the right words
in the right order on demand,
the hot blab of the poetry circuit.
So we promised him dinner,
publicity, and a powerful pull
at the punch bowl. We would have
thrown in Italy, rumba lessons, bought
him exclusive, elusive martyr rights
if only he'd come, read his poems
for our little group, disciplined
in nothing but midwest adoration.

He was a Name. What sneer
hadn't he perfected? The arched
eyebrow, the purple scarf, the right
of the rake's progress through
the field of ingénues swaying
before him: children of the corn
facing the blades of the combine.

Over dinner we talked poetry,
influences, whom he read.
His shortlist of favorites? He
and himself, as if Yeats never
put pen to paper. Shakespeare
wasn't Shakespeare, and poor Keats
never hatched a poorer nightingale.
Frost, Neruda, Rilke—forget it.

"No women?" we said, "Sappho,
Dickinson, Levertov?" He choked
on his fish.
                    Reader, lest I sound
out of joint, I offer up only
what memory shakes out,
and if memory shakes out bitter,
be assured it remains clear-eyed.

He diddled his fork, wiped
his mouth, then, surveying
the table and not finding what
he was looking for, looked down
as if conferring with his plate:
Where's the woman?

No, not a Barrett to banter
with his Browning—alter ego
and companion—but a gate
of female flesh, swung open, wide
and generous. A paltry wage
for genius, yes, but what can be
expected from volunteer work
done flat on the back and provided?

Sing, O Muse, the cockiness
of the Y chromosome: sole proprietor
of the poetry gene—that itch, that
flea strutting to the podium to be born.

He read from his "work in progress,"
shuffling, dropping papers, attending
diligently to the fuss of his scarf.
And I wish—for art and the poetry
we kept dangled before us, glittery

as the fruit of Tantalus because
we wanted it so bad—I wish
I could rewrite this story, saying
no one nodded off or walked out,
saying the big man's poems were enough
to fly us beyond judgment's orbit
to where the real stars burn. Their work,
more than bright enough to render the least of them
forgivable. I wish I could tell you that.

Wendy Barker

The Feminine Mystique

No, I hadn't heard of it. Ty was telling me everybody was talking about it, this Friedan woman. He had to read it for his class at Cal. Maybe I should read it. Yeah, why didn't I read it, and then he wouldn't have to, and I could write his paper for him. Easy for me. I said I didn't mind. Okay. When I finished reading the whole book he wanted to know what I thought. I wasn't sure. But I didn't have a hard time writing his paper. I just said things the way he'd say them, organized it all into paragraphs, made sure everything was correct. Did I like the book? I didn't know. Maybe my mother had been like the women Friedan wrote about—the problem that had no name. I didn't really want to talk about it, as long as the paper was good enough for him to turn in. And tonight—if I could stay with him, not have to go home.

Diane Wakoski

Love Letter Postmarked Von Beethoven

for a man I love
more than I should,
intemperance being something
a poet cannot afford

I am too angry to sleep beside you,
you big loud symphony who fell asleep drunk;
I try to count sheep and instead
find myself counting the times I would like to shoot you
in the back,
your large body
with its mustaches that substitute for love
and its knowledge of motorcycle mechanics that substitutes
for loving me;
why aren't you interested in
my beautiful little engine?
It needs a tune-up tonight, dirty with the sludge of
anger, resentment,
and the pistons all sticky, the valves
afraid of the lapping you might do,
the way you would clean me out of your life.

I count the times your shoulders writhe
and you topple over
after I've shot you with my Thompson Contender
    (using the .38-caliber barrel
      or else the one they recommend for shooting rattlesnakes).
I shoot you each time in that wide dumb back,
insensitive to me,

glad for the mild recoil of the gun
that relieves a little of my repressed anger
each time I discharge a bullet into you;
one for my father who deserted me and whom you masquerade as,
every night, when you don't come home
or even telephone to give me an idea of when to expect you;
the anguish of expectation in one's life
and the hours when the mind won't work, waiting
for the sound of footsteps on the stairs,
the key turning in the lock;
another bullet for my first lover,
a boy of 18,
        (but that was when I was 18 too)
who betrayed me and would not marry me.
You too, betrayer,
you who will not give me your name as even a token of affection:
another bullet,
and of course each time
the heavy sound of your body falling over in work boots,
a lumber jacket, and a notebook in which you write down
everything
but reality;
another bullet for those men
who said they loved me
and followed other women into their silky bedrooms
and kissed them behind curtains,
who offered toasts to other women,
making me feel ugly, undesirable;
anger, fury, the desire to cry or to shake you back
to the way you used to love me.
even wanted to,
knowing that I have no recourse,
that if I air my grievances you'll only punish me more
or tell me to leave,
and yet knowing that silent grievances

will erode my brain,
make pieces of my ability to love
fall off,
like fingers from a leprosied hand;
and I shoot another bullet into your back,
trying to get to sleep,
only wanting you to touch me with some gesture of affection;
this bullet for the bad husband who would drink late in bars
and not take me with him,
talking and flirting with other women
and who would come home, without a friendly word, and sleep
celibate next to my hungry body;
a bullet for the hypocrites;
a bullet for my brother who could not love me without guilt;
a bullet for the man I love who never listens to me:
a bullet for the men who run my country without consulting me;
a bullet for the man who says I am a fool to expect anyone to
listen to me;
a bullet for the man who wrote a love poem to me
and a year later threw it away, saying it was a bad poem.
If I were Beethoven, by now I'd have tried every
dissonant chord;
were I a good marksman, being paid to test this new Thompson
Contender, I'd have several dozen dead rattlesnakes lying
along the path already;
instead, I am ashamed of my anger
at you
whom I love
whom I ask for so much more than you want to give.
A string quartet would be too difficult right now.
Let us have the first movement of the Moonlight Sonata.
I will try counting the notes
instead of sheep.

Diane Wakoski

Filling the Boxes of Joseph Cornell

Aren't we nasty little people
looking at treasure boxes?
                    here is one having a pair of chocolate legs
                    in high heels,
                    a silver mirror,
                    a beef tongue, slightly purplish
                    and streaked like meat turning bad,
and only wanting to
change their contents;
fill them with ourselves?

            The structure of anger
            is repetition;
            tell him over and over you saw the girl he raped
            and killed, her face streaked purple
            large blotches on her breasts,
            part of the hand severed
            and thrown across the room,
            and over and over you tell him
            yelling at him about how you saw her and what he
            did, and how you hate him and how he took someone's
            life, and the structure of your anger
            is *only* repetition,
            or all the ugly things,
            over and over

                    (I'll say, "he hurt me,
                    he hurt me,"
                    over and over,

thinking about the assault,
trying to make it go away
out of my head
all memory of him leave me.

we are standing outside of a window displaying
electronic equipment. $100 for this small speaker,
$300 for this turn table. $400 for this amplifier.
You can scarcely contain yourself, wanting all these beautiful
square boxlike parts that will make sounds slip into your
ears like a beautiful pair of hands.

When I used to go to the movies on Friday nights with my
mother and sister in Whittier, California, we used to see the
previews of coming attractions, and even though I knew
that we went to the movies every week-end, I
could scarcely sit in my seat,
wanting so physically to be there, seeing the new movie
in color perhaps with Betty Grable wearing chocolate colored
stockings and sitting in her dressing room looking at
the mirror, while the rich ugly man
brought her flowers and the poor handsome
man waited outside.

Whose tongue was hanging out for her?

Your tongue hanging out for new hi-fi equipment.
No matter where we see the scenes, we are structuring
the parts we like, putting them into little stagelike boxes
of our own, with out own additions—
        some ostrich feathers,
        a silver inkwell,
        a dime bank, a photo of a countess,
        a graduation certificate;

fill them ourselves, as if the world had no artistry,
no sense of placement, no choice
settling things where they were settled.
        The old man, my kind father-in-law,
        saying after having painted watercolors for 20 years,
        little landscapes and vases of flowers,
        getting up at 5 in the morning to go into the city
        and sketch an hour before work
        and whose only problem was that he had little
            talent—
        though skill was something he knew about
        and tried to perfect–
        he said, as we drove through the country,
        that he always changes the landscape when he paints
            it,
        because there is no good arrangement in nature,
        only he always changed it
        by putting in the same barn,
        the same two rocks,
        and the same boat, even when there was no water,
        the boat then being disguised as a bush

Aren't we nasty little people,
looking at boxes, never accepting what is there,
always putting in our own arrangements?

    The structure of anger
    is repetition. We are angered by people trying to
    arrange our lives for us–no structure we
    build being suitable for all others,
    the argument about whether this war is worse than
        all other wars—two pacifists militantly fighting about
    when it's right to kill, another pacifist
    saying how killing can only be evil,

but letting his parents destroy him, kill him
with softness and tenderness and kindness
at an early age, and now he is doing it to his own child,
and she in anger, even as a 10-year-old, lashing
out in anger, not learning to read, not learning to
talk, not learning to keep herself clean, and secretly
knowing what she is doing,
killing,
        this repetition, over and over

The same poem, the same life, the same destructive relationships,
relating the color—if it's blue
    I am blue
    I am blue as a blues singer
    I am blue in the face from saying the same things over
        & over
    I am blue because of you and what you've done to me
    I am blue because it was my favorite color as a baby
    (it didn't take much to teach me
    that my parents wanted a boy
    and the best adjustment I could make was to
    like blue)

Little boy blue, come blow your horn
Sheep's in the meadow, cow's in the corn.

Repetition is the structure of anger.

You keep saying something over and over
and it goes away
or you go away from it,
ultimately being bored with too much of a good thing.

There is a man who keeps making boxes
and putting new and strange and beautiful things in them.

a map of all the currents of all the oceans in the world
and a silver instrument of steering a ship
sometimes ladies' objects; sometimes men's.
Never the same; never a repetition of subject,
but always the box, over and over.

Repetition is what structures our lives . . . Where we find a unity
we find a work of art, some sense,
something we call a life?

For years I have been repeating formulae I learned to
keep my devils away; and now I don't have any devils, but I say
the same formulae when angels are around
and
of course
they go away too.

The structure of repetition is one that makes songs
and dances and boxes
        I don't want to repeat myself.
        It seems to be the only way of getting a point across
            though

Across the ocean I know someone who's repeating himself
and who repeated himself
    just as when someone doesn't hear you, they will
    ask you to repeat what you said,
    or there might be a repeat broadcast of something we liked
    on the radio, or you might have to repeat a course you
    failed in school or when you belch you are
    repeating your food.
    Mainly,
    repetition is for learning or for fear

Have I repeated myself enough? Little boy blue,

that's you.
I never turned out to be Little Boy Blue,
just a woman who likes blue a lot,
even the blues.
If I repeat your name three hundred times in a row
it will begin to sound absurd;
if I replayed our life together, all the scenes three hundred
times they too would seem absurd–but everything in the world
would, under such conditions

What I want most of all is to repeat your name
until you become something real,
not a fantasy.
What I want is a structure of repetition
that makes me angry,
makes me strong
(because, as Martha said, anger is a stronger emotion
in our culture).
For once,
I'd like to look at the artist's velvet-lined box
and enjoy his world.
My tongue is not large and purple and streaked with rot,
as is his beef tongue.
Mine has smaller,
different things to say.

It is a mark of determination
or stupidity
to repeat your mistakes.

George Ella Lyon

Mary

When you were young
and lanky, graceful
bones visible, your wide
mouth and bright hair
made a vivid frame
for your voice.
On either side of you
dark-suited men
played guitars and sang,
their fingers dancing.

Your instrument
was that body.
A woman, you carried
the melody or high harmony,
the descant, or low
weave of thirds and fifths
and beauty too.
You had to be beacon
virgin, siren
little girl, and vamp.
It comes to us at birth,
this mantle—
no way to step onstage
without reference to it.

So you worked it,
shaking your hair
like a flag in the wind.

You were an actress after all.
No use to wear the mantle
like some ratty carpet remnant
when you could perfect
that dazzling twirl
managers, photographers,
and audiences swooned for.
It wasn't just the erotic
heat you bore like any torch
singer, but the shiny
energy advertising tomorrow
that rides a young woman's flesh.

In fact, you were already
a mother, your daughter
kept out of view. A grand-
mother now—heavy, clear
lines gone—you've survived
back surgeries, leukemia, bone
marrow transplant. Peter
and Paul, gray, thick and bald
betray nothing. But you!
Some folks can't hear you
now because of what they
see, since your look was your
sound was your message round
and round the spindle
of image and desire.

Yes, your voice is lower, brassier
but Peter's and Paul's have
grown raspy, too, yet no website
bears their distorted pictures
like ones of you I found captioned
"Repulsive" and "Jabba the Hutt."

And you the same woman who helped
rally the "I Have a Dream" march,
who with mother and daughter
went to jail for protesting apartheid,
who gave your voice to changing
the times, to turning a nation.

These days you come onstage
with a cane and wavy sparse
after-chemo hair, bearing another
torch for us, the light of believing
anyway and laughing, the wise
slow steps of carrying it on.

Robert Bonazzi

César Vallejo Died On A Rainy Night

I died walking in cold rain—I recall it exactly—
those familiar Parisian alleys, these worn shoes . . .

When I died I was walking wet night alleys,
dreaming of that face, her placid flesh—
no one else had travelled there . . .

When I died—I remember it well—those staring eyes,
smooth remote stones, underwater, alone . . .

The drenched sky emptied without regret—
shoes stripped off, pockets picked & flattened
over smooth stones, over dangerous waters.

III.

ACCELERATION

the times a changing

Leon Stokesbury

The Day Kennedy Died

Suppose that on the day Kennedy died
you had a vision. But this was no inner movie
with a discernible plot or anything like it.
Not even very visual when you get down
to admitting what actually occurred.
About two-thirds through 4th period
Senior Civics, fifteen minutes before
the longed-for lunchtime, suppose you
stood up for no good reason—no reason
at all really—and announced, to the class
and to yourself, "Something. . . coming. I
can see. . . something. I can see. I. . ."

And that was all. You stood there: blank.
The class roared. Even Phyllis Hoffpaur, girl
most worshipped by you from afar that year,
turned a vaguely pastel shade of red
and smiled, and Richard Head, your best friend,
Dick Head to the chosen few, pulled you down
to your desk whispering, "Jesus, man! Jesus
Christ!" Then you went numb. You did not know
what had occurred. But thirty minutes later,
when Stella (despised) Vandenburg, teacher
of twelfth grade English, came sashaying
into the lunchroom, informing, left and right,
as many digesting members of the student body
as she could of what she had just heard,
several students began to glance back at you,
remembering what you'd said. A few pointed,

whispering to their confederates, and on that
disturbing day they moved away in the halls.
Even Dick Head did not know what to say.

In 5th period Advanced Math, Principal
Crawford played the radio over the intercom
and the school dropped deeper into history.
For the rest of that day, everyone moved away—
except for the one moment Phyllis Hoffpaur
stared hard, the look on her face asking,
assuming you would know, "Will it be ok?"

And you did not know. No one knew.
Everyone staggered back to their houses
that evening aimless and lost, not knowing,
certainly sensing something had been
changed forever. *Silsbee High forever!*
That is our claim! Never, no never!
Will we lose our fame! you often sang.
But this was to be the class of 1964,
afraid of the future at last, who would select,
as the class song, Terry Stafford's *Suspicion.*
And this was November—even in Texas
the month of failings, month of sorrows—
from which there was no turning.
It would be a slow two-months slide until
the manic beginnings of The British Invasion,
three months before Clay's ascension to the throne,
but all you saw walking home that afternoon
were the gangs of gray leaves clotting the curbs
and culverts, the odors of winter forever
in the air: cold, damp, bleak, dead, dull:
dragging you toward the solstice like a tide.

Jim Daniels

Soul Sacrifice

Mike Clonski was my friend. He sat one row over from
me in Earth Science. He did the daily school announce-
ments, which meant he got to choose the music that
played in the hallways while we changed classes. Once
I gave him my Woodstock album and asked him to play
"Soul Sacrifice" by Santana—a great song to change
classes to. I recommend it highly, that manic guitar echo-
ing down the long hallways of Fitzgerald High where all
1,236 of us bopped a little, jiggled a little, moved quicker
in spite of wanting to move slower because *Soul Sacrifice*,
for crying out loud!—Earth Science was science for those
not going to college, not that it provided information
more useful than biology or chemistry for the average
future factory rat, but having *earth* in it made it sound
more practical. After all, we *lived* on earth. Why didn't
they just call it Earth? They didn't call biology *Biology
Science*. Clonski arrived late to class the days he did
announcements. He was a music head and a pot head and
just about any kind of head you could name. He had a big
old curly head of hair he parted in the middle hippie style
because he was one of two hippies at Fitzgerald High
School, the other being Jim Tanicki, who was a freak in
every sense of the word, the tallest kid in the school with
another six inches of wild curly blonde hair on top of it.
He and Clonski were best friends, letting their freak flags
fly. My father still cut my hair. Too short, and we fought
over it. I would surprise everyone, even me, and go on to
college. Bonnie Melkan sat right in front of me. Bonnie
was simply beautiful, her long hair *nearly* down to her ass,

and her ass that day, slightly revealed by her hip hugger jeans as she bent over her seat—and as "Soul Sacrifice" wound down and we sat in our seats wailing for class to begin, Mr. Chubbell's bald, skeletal zombie-like head smiling at Bonnie as he did every single day though he smiled at no one else ever and resented teaching Earth Science because he was a physicist who should only be teaching the smart kids and Bonnie knew what she knew because like all of us she was no dummy so she sort of smiled back, then looked away and got her A but that day she could not help herself and her ass shook a little in the seat, and I was swimming with her ass crack, neither of us distracted by books that day—they were so heavy, we were so light with "Soul Sacrifice." I knew how hot the earth's core was for ten seconds. When Clonski showed up, his hair wagging like a happy dog, and plopped down across from me, he handed back my album that gave me all the facts I would ever need, and I unfolded it at my desk to take a quick look at the large photo of the naked people swimming and Bonnie Melkan turned around while Mr. Chubbell was taking roll and it looked like she was going to say something, but she didn't, her eyes meeting mine above the album cover and because Bonnie knew what she knew she gave me a smile that exploded my head like a cherry bomb, then turned back to say "Here" and Clonski looked over and smiled and rolled his enormous eyes at me like something out of astronomy, like a constellation we all knew but had no name for.

David Kirby

The Summer of the Cuban Missile Crisis

Dickie asks if we are hungry, and Art and I say yeah, sure,
        so he pulls into the Walt Whitman Service
Plaza near Camden and there, in front
                of the very Howard Johnson's where we're going
to eat, is a bus with painted fire blazing down its sides

and above it, in letters two feet high, the words JAMES
        BROWN AND THE FAMOUS FLAMES, and I think,
righhht, this is it: I am sixteen years old,
                I have my first paying job, I'm traveling
across country with two guys who are older and cooler than I am

yet who seem to accept me as their equal and if that's not enough,
        now I'm going to meet Mr. I Got You, Mr. Let a Man
Get Up and Do the Popcorn (Part 1), Mr. I Break
                Out in a Cold Sweat, the Hardest Working Man
in Show Business, James Brown himself.

Dickie is Dickie Biles, and Art is Arthur Kennedy,
        and they both go to the LSU Medical
School in New Orleans, so it's no problem for them
                to swing through Baton Rouge
on their way to Massachusetts and give me a ride to the camp

where we've all been hired to work that summer, even though
        they're the camp doctors and I'm just
a kid and a mere archery/riflery counselor at that. Dickie
                is not only full of fun and ideas
but is also one of those people who knows someone

in every town, so whenever we get tired or hungry,
            we pull over, Dickie gets out
his address book, and within five minutes,
                        we're turning into the driveway
of one of his friends, including a guy in Lynchburg, Virginia

named Stump who'd just finished a pizza and a six pack
            when Dickie calls and who keeps staring
at Dickie in disbelief and asking me
                        and Art, "What did you say
your name was?" Then there's Dickie's friend in Arlington

who has a beagle who sings along when Dickie plays
            the piano, and a third friend in Chevy Chase
who had played bagpipes for the Trinity College Drum
                        & Fife Corps and who says,
"Watch this, the neighbors hate it" and goes into his back yard

and lights into "McPherson's Lament," and sure enough,
            all these old people come out
of their houses and said, "Now cut that out" and "That's it,
                        I'm calling the cops"—
pretty heady stuff for a provincial sixteen-year-old, but nothing

compared to the prospect of meeting Mr. Try Me.
            Mr. Stand Up I Feel Like a Sex Machine, Mr. Please,
Please, Please, the unquestioned King of Funk.
                        Of course, he's not there:
JB had gone ahead, probably by limo, but the Famous Flames

are all inside the Howard Johnson's, waiting for their food
            and looking extremely hip in their
shiny suits and skinny ties. Dickie and Art and I sit at the counter
                        and place our orders, mine
being a chicken salad on toast and a strawberry soda made

with peppermint ice cream, but while we're waiting,
        a guy sitting a few stools down
from us begins to pitch a real fit. "This malted tastes
              terrible," he says, only
he pronounces it "mwalted" and holds up his malt glass

and waves it at the counter girl, who's my age and extremely
        pretty, and says, "There's something
wrwong heh, something very wrwong," and he keeps waving
           the glass at the counter girl and trying
to get her to taste the malt, and by now she's nearly in tears,

and the guy's kicking up such a ruckus that even the Famous
        Flames have stopped being cool and are looking
our way. It's probably just a soapy glass,
          if anything, but the guy keeps
going on and on, and finally Dickie gets up and goes over

and says, "Richard Biles, M. D." (which isn't quite true,
        since he still has a year of medical school
left), "may I see that glass, please? Hmm, yes.
          Yes," says Dickie, sniffing the malt
suspiciously, "just as I feared." He puts one thumb on

the guy's eyelid and peers in. "Sir, you have been poisoned.
        Someone has put poison in your
malted milkshake. And there's no cure."
          The guy stares at Dickie for a second,
eyes bulging with terror, and goes, "Gaaahh!" and runs out

into the parking lot, clutching his neck with both hands.
        The counter girl bursts out laughing,
and so do the famous Flames, who gave each other
          complicated handshakes
and tell Dickie he's all right and autograph a Howard

Johnson's place mat for me, and as we go out the door,
        I look back, and the counter girl puts
a little kiss on her finger tips and blows it at me, though
                I'm so surprised that I don't catch it
and berate myself later for having been so clumsy and stupid,

and off we go to Cape Namequoit in Orleans, Massachusetts,
        where Dickie and Art pass out aspirin
and bandaids and calamine lotion, and I teach kids not
                to shoot themselves and even hit
the target from time to time, and the summer goes by in a hazy blur,

the best thing about it having already happened
        at the very beginning. Now obviously I still think
about those days, but when I do, I think
                less of Dickie Biles and the Famous
Flames and the poisoned guy and the pretty counter girl

and more of Art Kennedy, who was one of those big, bearish guys
        whose solid calm was a welcome contrast
to Dickie's excitability and my provincial self-doubt and who
                never said much the whole trip but looked
out the car window a lot and whom I now associate with the other,

more celebrated Kennedys: John and Bobby, who would be
        shot dead in a few years, and tragic, lucky Teddy,
who would drown poor Mary Jo Kopechne in a pond not far from
                the camp where we worked and then
go scot free, whereas anyone else would have done serious time.

There was something in Art's gaze as he looked out
        and the landscape changed and the shadows grew long
and the sun went down over Lynchburg and Arlington
                and Chevy Chase. The summer sped by
more quickly than anyone could have imagined, and with it came

the Cuban missile crisis and, soon, rumors about John and Marilyn,
        and then Oswald and the grassy knoll
and the Freedom Riders the summer after that, and then
              the war and hippies and acid
and the Summer of Love, and then rumors about Bobby

and Marilyn, and then Sirhan Sirhan and Malcolm X
        and the police riots in Chicago
and the three days of Woodstock and the bridge
           at Chappaquiddick, all of it
springing from that sad, gaudy amalgam of touch football

and nooky and Harvard diplomas and boat races off Hyannisport
        and conspiracies and mob connections
and horsedrawn carriages going up Pennsylvania Avenue
           to the sound of muffled drums.
What I tell myself is that Art was the brother who got away,

who turned his back on that whole bright, shining family, its blood
        hot with poison even in those innocent days,
though no one could have known it at the time.
          He was the smart Kennedy, the one who didn't
say anything because he knew no one would believe him.

Dede Fox

California Dreaming, LA 1966

Dad made sales calls.
I gawked from tour bus windows,
screamed through amusement park rides,
snapped my Instamatic in movie studios.

Under fading skies, we dined
al fresco with his friends in Bel Air,
perched on wrought iron chairs,
my eyes averted from the naked
statue that peed water into the pool.
Their daughter, three years older than my fifteen,
had a fiancé, a graying movie executive.
We were a long way from Bellaire…Texas.

One night we cruised Sepulveda and Sunset,
scanned flashing signs. We stopped.
Dressed in a hot pink granny dress
I had struggled to sew on Mother's old
machine, which knotted thread, tight
as my adolescent emotions, I jumped out,
shaking the sleeves sewn in backwards,
but I tossed back my shiny straightened
hair, and smiled at our adventure,
our goal to get into Whiskey a Go Go.

Percussion and bass guitar throbbed from the doorway.
My heart raced as Dad shouted to someone in the shadows.
When he turned to me, creases lined his high forehead.
He shook his head. Neon flashed orange and green,

strobed across our faces. He studied me.
I shrugged. We threaded our way
through streets crowded with beaded hippies.
We'd do Disneyland together tomorrow.
Not much time left.

Martín Espada

Public School 190, Brooklyn 1963

The inkwells had no ink.
The flag had 48 stars, four years
after Alaska and Hawaii.
There were vandalized blackboards
and chairs with three legs,
taped windows, retarded boys penned
in the basement.
Some of us stared in Spanish.
We windmilled punches
or hid in the closet to steal from coats
as the teacher drowsed, head bobbing.
We had the Dick and Jane books,
but someone filled in their faces
with a brown crayon.

When Kennedy was shot,
they hurried us onto buses,
not saying why,
saying only that
something bad had happened.
But we knew
something bad had happened,
knew that before
November 22, 1963.

W. E. Butts

The Industrial Diamonds of 1964

That spring I dropped out of college
and took a factory job back in the small town
I had been so certain I'd never return to,
and stood at my task of gears and wheels,
where I cursed—or it could have been prayer—
through each shift's final hour.

In the lunch room, old-timers
mocked the new hires, argued
about Kennedy, Oswald, and Ruby,
and how those damn Cubans were
behind it all. That was why we had
to stay in Vietnam, and to hell
with the hippies and Commies.

We were grinding circular saw blades,
fitting them with industrial diamonds,
and each hundred-thousandth inch meant
a paycheck we might live with, something
to take every Friday to the bank and tavern,
place of dimmed lights, twenty-five cent draughts,
baseball scores, boxing matches,
horse racing odds, the two-dollar-bet,
and a chance few of us believed in.

I think of those men now, and remember
our labor, the metal shavings I washed off
my hands and arms each night at the sink,

the ache of shoulders and wrists, the blessing
of sleep, the pre-dawn wakening to rock and roll
music playing on the clock radio,
the gem-like glitter of a few last stars,
and then the turbulent and risen sun.

Bryce Milligan

Four-Stroke

If ever you spent much quality time on the hurricane deck
of a trusted motorcycle then had to give it up—trading
it in, say, for a station wagon to haul around your rock
band or maybe pay a tuition bill or buy an engagement
ring—then you'll recognize the symptoms of the syn-
drome: involuntary if slight twists of the wrist, muscle
memory that leans into a curve, the tendency to roll down
the car window with the A/C on, prompting your wife/
kids/partner to ask if something is wrong—every time
you pass a rider in your family minivan or SUV or silent
little electric leaf blowing down the highway, and it dawns
on you that you never really fell out of love with that old
Honda 305 or the chopped metal-flake green Triumph
650 or even the minibike you built with your dad, with
its angle-iron frame (that's how you learned to weld), its
wheel barrow tires, bicycle handlebars, and the 3.5 horse-
power Briggs & Stratton four-stroke former lawn mower
engine that your father insisted you must rebuild before
he would even entertain the idea of letting you spend your
allowance on a real centrifugal clutch, and so you spent
weeks figuring out how to take it apart, washing each
part in gasoline, and naming the parts—ah, the naming
of parts: there seemed to be hundreds but it was only a
few dozen—as you laid them out neatly on a sheet of
cardboard on the garage floor: piston and rings and rod,
camshaft and timing chain, valves and lifters, ball bearing
races, carburetor needles and springs and floats and ports,
and the beautiful gleaming crankshaft—and what was of
importance to most third grade minds was simply blown

away by the burning desire to know the name and function of every part and to use the seemingly ancient tools to bore the cylinder by hand, grind the valves by hand, clean each carburetor orifice by hand, and replace every part correctly in relationship to the others so that like your father cleaning his rifle beneath a jeep on the beach at Iwo Jima you could do it from memory in the dark, and your father watched, advised and consoled you when it did not start the first time or the second time or the fifteenth time you took it apart and put it back together as third grade became fifth grade until finally the magic of mechanics worked and the engine roared and you danced a private jig in the twilight of the garage to the rhythm the engine puttered, bolted to its vibrating wooden base, as you sang "I've just seen a face, I can't forget the time or place, where we just met" and you were startled to find that you were as in love with that 3.5 horsepower, four-stroke Briggs & Stratton engine as you ever were with the girl with the Picasso pony tail who sat in the desk in front of you the day Kennedy died and with whom no one could even compare until you met the love of your life a decade later—*that* kind of obsessive love, the kind that led you to copy out by hand the *Encyclopaedia Britannica* article on trigonometry and damn near memorize the thing while barely understanding it just like you'd memorized the engine parts on the garage floor or her pony tail on that cold November morning without a clue as to what drove you to begin writing poetry of all things that very day—and when that kind of love was rewarded not only with the gift of a shiny new centrifugal clutch but the consequent gift of actual speed, as if you'd been gifted with the Wright Brothers' wings, speed, solitary, wind-making, hair-whipping, jacket-flapping speed, speed that would grow with one machine after another just as the bonds with your father would dissolve in the face of a war, so unlike his, that you could not agree to fight, speed that would carry you across deserts and mountains to the Haight, from Woody Guthrie to T.S. Eliot and back again, from the trinity of sex, drugs and guitars to that of blood, birth and the quietude you only glimpse now when the highway wind lashes eye and ear and arm as you watch some young man and his twenty-something old lady twist the throttle that churns the four stroke dream between his legs, accelerating, pulling away, leaving you with mere echoes of desire.

Jim Elledge

Duckling, Swan

In bunches bright as marigolds,
azaleas, bachelor's-
buttons, women outnumber men ten to one
on this drizzling morning's commuter,
women who have big hair, chit-
chat about the week's
Geraldos, glare my way as I board.

I admit it.

            In my black motorcycle jacket
I'm nothing like a god. Not
even close. In black toe to crown,
I'm more the demon dreamt than
trumpeting archangel floating
through a cumulus of Lady
Clairol creations, striding past
tips on P.C. muscle
exercises and the futures market.
Doing my best Jim Morrison,
I admit it: I love how, still glaring,
they steal peeks at my crotch.

As if it matters, I think of Terry
Herrick, the beautiful j.d. of Prather Jr.
High who grew hair before any of
us and showed off in the showers, who
curling an index finger, brought
cheerleaders to their knees,

who taught me how to inhale without
choking, who kept
Johnny Redman from kicking
my ass more times than I remember,
who pimped his mother, who was offed
by the St. Louis mob.

And then my hand touched
brings me back to the downpour, the rails
paralleling I-55, the minutes between
departure and arrival strung
out slow as a cello's moan,
to the other fiction, the one so real my
gut aches to bursting.

        A woman
across the aisle, abandoned by her
friends for the café car,
for the little girl's, for other
acquaintances seats away, draws her hand
back, leans over the aisle, and mouths,
Can I pet your leather?

Richard Wilbur

A Miltonic Sonnet for Mr. Johnson
on His Refusal of Peter Hurd's Official Portrait

Heir to the office of a man not dead
Who drew our Declaration up, who planned
Range and Rotunda with his drawing-hand
And harbored Palestrina in his head,
Who would have wept to see small nations dread
The imposition of our cattle-brand,
With public truth at home mistold or banned,
And in whose term no army's blood was shed,

Rightly you say the picture is too large
Which Peter Hurd by your appointment drew,
And justly call that Capitol too bright
Which signifies our people in your charge;
Wait, Sir, and see how time will render you,
Who talk of vision but are weak of sight.

6 January 1967

Sandra M. Gilbert

Her Last Sickness

(Sylvia Plath, d. 1963)

Sailing the long hot gulf
of her last sickness,
out past the whispering beach,
she saw the town lights dim.
What were those voices shouting in her head?
She was their sentence, they were hers.
Words ripped at her ribs
like multiplied hearts, until
she drowned in that intolerable pulse.

Now riding the slow tide
she's dumb as driftwood, sheds
her last light skins of thought
easily as October.
Mounting the great salt flow,
black with it, white with its foam,
she's picturesque—no more than a design
on the packed sand, hieroglyph
from another land.

Martín Espada

The Sign in My Father's Hands

for Frank Espada

The beer company
did not hire Blacks or Puerto Ricans,
so my father joined the picket line
at the Schaefer Beer Pavilion, New York World's Fair,
amid the crowds glaring with canine hostility.
But the cops brandished nightsticks
and handcuffs to protect the beer,
and my father disappeared.

In 1964, I had never tasted beer,
and no one told me about the picket signs
torn in two by the cops of brewery.
I knew what dead was: dead was a cat
overrun with parasites and dumped
in the hallway incinerator.
I knew my father was dead.
I went mute and filmy-eyed, the slow boy
who did not hear the question in school.
I sat studying his framed photograph
like a mirror, my darker face.

Days later, he appeared in the doorway
grinning with his gilded tooth.
Not dead, though I would come to learn
that sometimes Puerto Ricans die
in jail, with bruises no one can explain
swelling their eyes shut.

I would learn too that "boycott"
is not a boy's haircut,
that I could sketch a picket line
on the blank side of a leaflet.

That day my father returned
from the netherworld
easily as riding the elevator to apartment 14F,
and the brewery cops could only watch
in drunken disappointment.
I searched my father's hands
for a sign of the miracle.

Fleda Brown

Where She Was, Where He Was

She would have been writing Mrs. H.G.G. III,
over and over: baroque, block letters, calligraphy,
beside her homework list. She would have crossed
her legs and tucked her skirt beneath her thighs.

He would've been throwing snowballs. Then he would've
stomped in to the student center, where Kennedy
was debating Nixon on TV. He would have sat
with his friends a long time, electrified.

So much went on she never dreamed of, him
included. He, with his other life to get lived first.
Her, too. Who was Kennedy to her, then,
her heart already organized? The day the President

was shot, they said, separately, was leading
to this. They imagined signs they missed. They imagined
a single thought traveling along a bloody
vein until the day it burst, quick, broadcast

its lineage: she, headed down Duncan Street in the blue
Volkswagen; he, in the teacher's lounge when
the Special Ed teacher came in, ashen faced, beginning,
"No kidding....." " Look back, you knew how it was coming:

how neat she was, how precise with her handwriting
to hold back her desperate heart; how passionately
he loved Kennedy, how much they hoped for,
that ended while their story was on its way.

Beverly Matherne

Sons

When Junior came back from Spain in 66
at Christmas and didn't get killed in Vietnam,
Daddy cooked jambalaya and red beans
and invited the whole town to celebrate.

As the band played "Blueberry Hill,"
and Dixie Beer and mistletoe hung in the air,
June whisked me to the dance floor,
said how pretty and smart I was.
I drank his words, like everyone else,
wanted to know all about Spain, bull fights,
and long legs under red flamingo skirts.

Outside, firecrackers sparked
and shot, cherry bombs exploded,
cars blew their horns, bumper to bumper,
the levee blazed with bonfires,
all the way to New Orleans.

After midnight Mass, Mama
filled our bowls with andouille gumbo.
June headed home on a country lane.
His high school friend whizzed
skunk drunk in the other direction,
he didn't see June coming.
The sheriff broke the news.
Nobody cared for hot gumbo,
candied yams, or pralines.

The day after Christmas, mourners came.
We drank black coffee and stayed up
with June's body through the night.
Ernie Boy—just learning to play pitch and catch
with June—cried, threw up, and finally fell asleep
among the other little ones at the foot of the coffin.
My sister Shirley and I knelt beside it and prayed
and wondered whether everybody smelled it
but dared not say.

The next day, the pallbearer slid
the coffin in the mausoleum,
the way you slide a pan of bread into an oven.
The rain was cold and damp
and drenched the scarlet ribbons
on the great sprays of red roses at the wall.

That spring, Mama devoted herself to sorrow,
the way she did the stations of the cross
during Lent. She started checking out books
on death and suffering, wore black,
put sorrow in June's buggy, tucked his
quilt at its neck, and pushed the buggy
out of her bedroom, through the kitchen,
down the back steps, through cane fields,
and pastures, into swamp waters,
among wild orange irises.

She dredged the buggy from the swamp,
pushed it back to the house, down the driveway,
onto Grand Point Lane, to River Road ,
to St. Joseph's Church. She heaved,
she sweated, the wrinkles in her face stood taut.
She pulled the buggy up the church steps,

to the thick oak portal, up the aisle, to the altar,
did not genuflect, stared God straight in the eye,
and said *"Maudit fils de putain!*
You son of a bitch!"

The congregation froze,
she turned and waved her aims wildly,
"Au diable avec tous de vous autres!
To hell with all of you!" She banged
the buggy down the altar steps,
down the aisle to the *Pietá,*
who held the dead Christ in her arms;
in her supplicating hand,
a crystal rosary fractured swords
of light from the rose window above.

"Toi, toi. . . . you, you . . . ." Her voice cracked.
She hurled her arms around the neck
of the sorrowful mother, sobbed and sobbed ,
crumpled, as if suddenly shot.
Daddy ran to her, gathered her in his arms.
"It's OK, Mama. Let's go home, Mama."

Ten years later, melanoma tumors
covered Ernie Boy's body, and
Mama got restless again.
She got that wild look in her eyes
and searched closets, barns, and fields.
"What are you looking for?" asked Daddy.
"Le maudit boghei de bébé!
That goddamned buggy!" she said.

Dave Parsons

Austin Fire

*Memories from the day of the University of Texas Tower
shootings & the 100th anniversary of Scholz's Beer
Garden on August 1, 1966.*

Out of the cave
of European History class
I am struck
by squinting bright skies
strolling on the edge of the shadow
of the university tower shade
through the southeast campus quad
flip flopping to my Mustang
for my short drive to work
less than an hour before
student victim #1
will have fallen
in that very path.

I am traveling back now—
back to the pool—
down the hot tar entry
down the pebbled walkway
to Barton Springs
churning shadowy deep blue—
it's the blues—the gushing
blues 68 degrees year-round
offering a deadening numbness
making the youngest of skin
cadaver cold and this ordinary

workday, I am just another Life-
guard cut loose too soon.

And now—again
I am driving back
again back and away
away from the many
oblique precipices—falls
hidden undercurrents
jutting stones in the blinds
of the limestone aquifer
traveling back under and through
the towering pecan trees
just a short dash—and now again
Barton Springs Road—
The Rolling Stones—Can't Get No
Satisfaction. . . . everything
is heating up the day.

At Scholz's Garden
another grand spring
100 years of beer flowing
unjudgmentally through
the many unruly seasons
through the untold
joyous and unfettered
the anonymous generations
of the deemed and the damned
and all their wagging
Did you know(s). . . flying
around the ever blank
pages of air—air that receives, never
recording a single loving or gnashing word
of the produce of this imperfect garden
those sweaty hound dog days—I feel

that very air here again now—the gamey
smells of the Dutchman's beer garden
the carefree summer women
laughing braless in loose tie-dyes
swilling nickel Lone Stars
aiming flirtatious glances
then firing their deadly frank stares
swinging suntanned legs
to the juke box beats
Hey, Mr. Tambourine Man
play a song for me. . . all
positioned between
the two towers: the capital dome
topped with Lady Liberty
and UT's apex and bastille of education
and there now...and again—white puffs—

Sniper! Sniper!

Girls first! diving under
stone gray concrete tables
towering turquoise sky
ragged clouds
ripping the battle blue
drifting. . . mist like. . . hiding
momentarily gun site portals,
and our shade tree bunkers
fiery memories
embedded
like so many stray shots—

He was a crew cut
every mother's son
Boy Scout—Marine
sharpshooter

again all paths of mine—
In his last note to the world
Charles Whitman
requested an autopsy
with special consideration
to his brain. . . they found
a tiny, cloudy gray mass
of malignant tissue lined
in crimson—seems it's
always the smallest of embers.

Ai

Cuba, 1962

When the rooster jumps up on the windowsill
and spreads his red-gold wings,
I wake, thinking it is the sun
and call Juanita, hearing her answer,
but only in my mind.
I know she is already outside,
breaking the cane off at ground level,
using only her big hands.
I get the machete and walk among the cane,
until I see her, lying face-down in the dirt.

Juanita, dead in the morning like this.
I raise the machete—
what I take from the earth, I give back—
and cut off her feet.
I lift the body and carry it to the wagon,
where I load the cane to sell in the village.
Whoever tastes my woman in his candy, his cake,
tastes something sweeter than this sugar cane;
it is grief.
If you eat too much of it, you want more,
you can never get enough.

Paul Mariani

Brotherhood

Week one we went from sixteen
down to four & signed a kamikaze
pact between us not to quit.
I shaved my head so close that

Brother Paul, lecturing contra basso
on the dizzy driftings of Ulysses,
lifted his heavy brows & ceased
mid-dactyl to inquire of my lice.

Worse still the girls shunning
the four of us at parties, except
to stare as we served them drinks
or wrote them stupid verses on consignment.

Dogs too dogs avoided us. On campus
we had to don painter's caps
so preternaturally white even
the frat sadist with his whiskey-tumbler-

bulls-eye glasses could spot us
slouching across the tree-lined quad.
Each noon in one of the Quonset huts
on campus, a silverback gorilla

whacked an oak paddle up & down
the pink insides of our thighs.
The brothers tired, edgy, drunk.
Somehow we kept failing them.

To teach us, they used hurling sticks
across our cringing backsides: ash-hard,
curved, unsplittable. Pain so intense
Swinburne would have loved it.

Then, in mid-November, two hours
north in a dilapidated DeSoto:
a final weekend in the Catskills,
a huddled mass of eight arms

and as many legs gone beyond even
terror, exhausted, crawling through
a makeshift Via Dolorosa made up
of hay, beer, mud & horseshit.

And all for what? To say the Test
was passed? To listen moon-eyed
to initiation rites while a candle
on a cardboard altar sputtered?

So that, black-assed, we might limp
together down to the Greenleaf Bar
to swap stories of some mythic
predecessor's twelve-inch dong?

Here's to the two-year reign
of brotherhood forever, when we drank
until our shirts turned stiff with vomit.
When we stared in dismal stupefaction

as a brother fumbled with his date,
pleading for a blowjob, before he toppled
through a Harlem dancehall window.
Here's too to all those brothers

(including one sadist & a gorilla)
I ferried home each Friday night for nothing,
my brother's maladaptive brakeless Chevy
weaving back & forth across Manhattan

& the Bronx & Queens & Brooklyn & yes
even far-flung Staten Island, as we drifted
in the going round of wheels, and croaked
our hearts out to the empty hunter moon.

Richard Wilbur

For the Student Strikers

Go talk with those who are rumored to be unlike you,
And whom, it is said, you are so unlike.
Stand on the stoops of their houses and tell them why
You are out on strike.

It is not yet time for the rock, the bullet, the blunt
Slogan that fuddles the mind toward force.
Let the new sound in our streets be the patient sound
Of your discourse.

Doors will be shut in your faces, I do not doubt.
Yet here or there, it may be, there will start,
Much as the lights blink on in a block at evening,
Changes of heart.

They are your houses; the people are not unlike you;
Talk with them, then, and let it be done
Even for the grey wife of your nightmare sheriff
And the guardsman's son.

Written for the Wesleyan *Strike News*, Spring 1970

Ginny Lowe Connors

Optical Longings and Illusions

after Man Ray's piece in gouache, ink wash, and collage

Kinetic energy, write this down, Mr. Lewis said.
Chemical reactions. Zigzagging
through the corridors, I colored myself in.

The blackboard marked with chains
of letters, pluses and minuses clustering
around them. Circles, arrows. Longing

as loss of electrons. I saw constellations
missing their lucky stars, random lines
connecting emptiness to emptiness

across the dark night that had us surrounded.
Oh Mr. Lewis. Big ears and bow ties.
But there was something he knew—

dark matter. Chalk dust to me. My elemental
landscape was tending toward train tracks,
bridges suspended over air. Snow, melting.

Gravitational laws, he said. Changing forms.
Desk to desk, we passed back the mimeographs
with their purple ink. Inhaled their fumes

as if life alone was not enough to make us dizzy.
My best friend turned into a paper doll.
I watched her disappear. Solar flare.

W. E. Butts

The Other Language

Even her worried voice couldn't bring me
to answer the morning I hid in weeds
by the willow, some child's wrong idea
of his importance in the known and safe world.

Or perhaps it was a simple insistence
that my life mattered, that Mother would,
if I were really gone, after all miss her only son,
and regret those scoldings and rules.

But I came then to understand silence's bitter ache:
Mother turned away at the kitchen stove,
her darkened thoughts of a cold river
and drowned boy shadowing the sun-filled wall.

When Barbara Jean stepped from the line
of high school cheerleaders and leapt
into the brisk October air, calling out each letter
of my name, I ran gladly with the others
onto the field of end runs and tackles.

But what was announced over the PA that afternoon
we stood assembled at the gymnasium rally,
navy blazers and striped ties, our season's ritual
of recognition and awards: the President
shot and yes, dead, startled everyone quiet,
and then so strangely alone.

Once, I watched my father and his deaf mute friend
speak in the quick conversation of hand and fingers,
saw how it was we might become our own words,
and for years after Father died there were nights
I dreamt back his voice, but woke to my loud cries.

At Sunday Mass with my parents, I had believed
those mysterious Latin chants would save me,
held as certain scripture the impossible
stories of a favorite uncle, learned the lessons
of home and school, and listened for the truth,
as I do still, of who we are that has not been said.

David Jauss

Beauty

*The inside of his head was so beautiful, I tried
to hold the top of his head down.*
      —Jacqueline Kennedy Onassis

There was no time, no sense of before
or after, and its absence was filled
with the astonishing rose-pink rings

of his memory and passion.
There was no horror either, not yet,
only that beauty coiling around a fact

so large there was nothing she could do
but try to hold it in her hands . . .
Then time was back, a waterfall

crashing on rocks, and she was crawling
out of her seat toward the Secret
Service agent whose eyes were wild

with history. She was trying to disappear
into action, leave thought and feeling
behind her forever. But the reporter's question

hit her like an assassin's bullet
and she was back in the limousine,
cheers and waving hands

flanking their passage, a bouquet of roses
on her lap. Then the sudden stop
in the small talk, the recoil

of his last word, and once again she saw
her husband's head open up
like a strange flower . . .

And when she answered
she raised her hands, so beautiful
and small, to the top of her own skull.

Alice Friman

Dallas

1.

Home from Texas a week
and the sky still sagging, sodden
as a throwaway mattress left at the curb.
By rights the clouds should settle in
northeast of here over Klanville, Indiana,
where they've got the sheets to fit.

But what's all this got to do
with Texas and a city built to look good
from the highway? One concrete monolith
trimmed in day-glow green. And towers
of erection glass rising from the flat belly
of the plains like the Sons of Silicon,
but standing apart, keeping a distance
as if shouldering together for a skyline
would belie their history. Like when
the news got out about Texas: land of
land deals, and white guys only. So they came.
Bowie the slave smuggler out of Louisiana
packing a steel-edged hangover. Young Travis
from Alabama, running away from a murder
and letting a black man hang for it.
And Old Man Crockett, the politician, down
in the opinion polls already, with twelve
Tennessee boys who hadn't changed underwear
in a year, hot-eyed kids and hustlers
not knowing all they were doing

was trying out for the John Wayne part,
too big for life but riding the range again—
kingpins of parking lots and blowing papers
and not a soul in sight.

2.

There are no more books
in the Texas Book Depository on the comer
or Elm and Houston. No sign of Dick and Jane
or Little Sally, pigeon-toed in Mary Janes,
or Mother, aproned for life,
except for the display of Scott Foresman cartons
in the corner by the sixth-floor window
where they said he stashed the carbine
made in Italy, serial #2766, a real
bargain—$21.45 through the U.S. mails—
then, hurtling down the steps four at a time,
bought a Coke, fooled a cop,
hit the sidewalk and ran. You remember—
that day of the pink suit, the pillbox hat.

Eight days ago I stood where he stood.
The window so big you could swan dive
into that day again—open car, everyone waving.
America, young enough to break out in pimples.
Another *High Noon* it was. Another Hollywood
once upon a time—Camelot's King Arthur
and the Lone Star playing Russian roulette
at the round table. The skyscrapers
standing around like extras at Ruby's place,
slit-eyed in mirrored glasses, waiting
and apart, as if they had nothing to do with it.

IV.

ENACTMENTS

people get ready

C. K. Williams

King

1

A tall, handsome black man, bearded, an artist, in nineteen sixty-eight,
      in Philadelphia,
you're walking down Market Street two days after Martin Luther King's
      murder
on your way to the memorial service scheduled that morning near the
      Liberty Bell.
Thirty years later, and I can still picture you there: you're walking fast,
      preoccupied,
when suddenly a police car swerves over the curb in front of you, block-
      ing your way.

And I can see the two policemen, both white, cold, expressionless, glar-
      ing at you:
a long moment passes, then I see you looking over your shoulder, turn-
      ing away,
moving towards the street, to the back of the squad car, passing behind it
      off the curb,
around it to the sidewalk on the other side and continuing down Market
      again,
to Nineteenth, then right to Rittenhouse Square where someone's waiting
      for you.

When you see the person (he's white, like the policemen), you don't say
      anything;
though you'd made an appointment not an hour ago to go to the service
      together,

you don't even glance at him again until he runs after you, calling for
     you to wait.
You stop to talk to him then, but only long enough to tell him in a harsh,
     low voice
everything that had happened with the policemen, then a few hard sen-
     tences more.

                                    2

Maybe my trying to relive this with you should stop there; this after all is
     your story,
but something still feels unresolved between us, as so much does in our
     culture.
I've heard black friends say that in some ways race matters were easier
     then,
at least then the prejudice was out in the open, you knew where you
     were:
even the police were only the most visible edge of a hardly covert white
     racism.

But if the police were a symbol of something else, they were brutal
     enough at it.
You could, if you were black, man or woman, be beaten to death by po-
     licemen.
You could, at a cop's whim, be arrested for "disturbing the peace," or "re-
     sisting arrest,"
which meant you'd done nothing, but had been battered badly enough
     for it to show,
necessitating if not an excuse then a reason, which incidentally added to
     your sentence.

Back then, too, even if you could afford a good lawyer, who might get
     you off,

if the police were angry enough, you had reason to fear that in the bus
        from jail
to the courtroom, you'd be raped, gang-raped, and no one would dare say
        a thing.
All that had to have come to your mind as you stood, that idling squad
        car before you,
the cops inside it with their clubs and guns, impassive, their eyes challenging,
        hard.

                                    3

They'd have known when they'd spotted you where you were going;
        everyone was.
And they'd have seen that you were confident, full of yourself: an "uppity
        nigger."
However they'd have put it to themselves, they'd have believed that by in-
        sulting you
they could denigrate King with you, debase what he'd stood for, demon-
        strate to you
that if you thought he had released you from the trap of history you were
        deluded.

But there would have been even more they'd have wanted to be sure you
        understood,
were ready to break their fists on you, maim or kill you so that you'd un-
        derstand:
that their world would prevail, that authority, power, and absolute physi-
        cal coercion
with no ethical dimension whatsoever must and will precede all and re-
        solve all
and break everything down again and again into an unqualified domin-
        ion of force.

All that would have passed between you in an instant, what came next,
     though,
would have driven their rage to a level where you knew the situation
     might explode:
it was their suspicion, and your certainty, that even if they did apparently
     intimidate you,
they couldn't make you renounce in yourself the conviction of your
     moral worth,
the inextinguishable truth that would supersede even what might seem
     submission.

4

Wasn't that what would have made you know you'd have to turn and go
     around them?
Surely your fury outstripped your fear, but didn't you make a truce with
     them, and a wager?
The truce was your walking away and their acceptance of that as a sign of
     compliance;
the wager, on their part, was that in your pretense of capitulation there'd
     be uncertainty,
that one day you'd have to forgive yourself for your humiliation, and
     wouldn't be able to.

And wasn't the wager on your side that though you might be hurt by your
     seeming yielding,
the lesion of your doubt, your shame and possible self-accusations would
     be outweighed
by knowing that nothing would have justified letting them exert their
     thuggery on you,
that, no matter what they believed, they wouldn't, couldn't have negated
     your anger?
But wouldn't your surrender have scorched you? Wasn't that what you
     were saying to me?

Don't tell me you know what I feel, and don't give me that crap about being
        with us,
you wouldn't know how to be with us, you don't know the first thing about
        us.
For three hundred years we've coddled you, protected your illusions of in-
        nocence,
letting you go on thinking you're pure: well you're not pure, you're the
        same as those pigs.
And please, please, don't tell me again you can understand because you're
        a Jew.

5

A black man, a white man, three decades of history of remembering and
        forgetting.
The day was Good Friday: after a long winter, the first warm, welcoming
        odors of spring.
People flowed to Independence Hall Park from all directions, everyone
        was subdued;
if there were tensions, they were constrained by our shared grief; we held
        hands.
The night before, though, in some cities there were riots: gunfire, sol-
        diers, buildings burning.

Sometimes it's hard to know why they stopped: I often think if I were
        black in America,
I might want to run riot myself with the sheer hypocritical unendingness
        of it all:
a so-called politics of neglect, families savaged, communities fractured
        and abandoned.
Black man, white man: I can still see us, one standing stricken, the other
        stalking away;
I can still feel your anger, feel still because it's still in me my helpless de-
        spair.

And will you by now have been able to leave behind the indignities and
        offense
of both halves of that morning? Isn't that what we're supposed to do in
        our country;
aren't we given to believe our wounds will heal, our scars fade, our in-
        sults be redeemed?
Later, during the service, when the "overcome" anthem was sung, I
        started to cry;
many others in the crowd around were crying, black and white, but I
        couldn't see you.

Wendy Barker

Teaching *Uncle Tom's Children*

He was the only other honky in the room. But wasn't.
Blond natural. Was his mother or his dad white or black?
Kid played the best sax in town and only fourteen. Sax
so sweet and cool the moon rose cream over the hills and
stars broke the fog. He didn't talk much. Neither did I,
that first Black Lit class any of us taught. I didn't know
what to put on the board. Erased everything I'd written
before, but the erasers were full of dust from the chalk.
The blackboard turned powdery, a blur, clouded. We
moved on through *Nigger, Black Boy, Native Son.* Not
a kid caused trouble. Small sounds, fingers flipping the
white pages of the paperbacks I collected and stacked in
the corner cupboard after class. Slap of gum stretching
in and out of a mouth, hard sole of a shoe on the floor,
scraping the surface, an emery board. And the train, track
barely a block away, the train running the whole length
of the San Francisco Bay, cry moving ahead of it, toward
us, that wail.

Alan Shapiro

Between Assassinations

Old court. Old chain net hanging in frayed links from the rim,
The metal backboard dented, darker where the ball
For over thirty years has kissed it, the blacktop buckling,
The white lines nearly worn away. Old common ground
Where none of the black men warming up before the basket
Will answer or even look in my direction when I ask
If I can run too, the chill a mutual understanding,
One of the last we share, letting me join them here,
If nowhere else, by not letting me forget I don't belong.

Old court. Old courtesy, handshake, exchange of names,
In the early days of bussing, between assassinations,
Before our quaint welcoming of them had come to seem,
Even to ourselves, the haughty overflow of wealth
So thoroughly our own we didn't need to see it.
Old beautiful delusion in those courtly gestures
That everything now beyond our wanting just to play
Was out of bounds, and we were free between the white lines
Of whatever we assumed we each of us assumed.

Old court, old dream dreamed by the weave, the trap,
The backdoor pass. Old fluid legacy, among the others,
That conjures even now within our bodies and between them
Such a useless, such an intimate forgetting, as in the moment
When you get a step on your defender and can tell
Exactly by how another man comes at you
Where your own man is and, without looking, lob the ball
Up in the air so perfectly as he arrives that
In a single motion he can catch and finger roll it in.

Old court, old dwindling ceasefire, with no hope of peace,
That we silently turn away from when the game is over,
Hurrying back (as if believing contact meant contagion)
To our separate tribes, to the cleansing fires of what,
Despite ourselves, we momentarily forgot:
Old love, old news, old burning certitudes we can't
Stoke up or hot enough, yet won't stop ever stoking
Until whatever it is we think we are anneals
And toughens into an impenetrable shield.

Toi Derricotte

Blackbottom

When relatives came from out of town,
we would drive down to Blackbottom,
drive slowly down the congested main streets
      —Beubian and Hastings—
trapped in the mesh of Saturday night.
Freshly escaped, black middle class,
we snickered, and were proud;
the louder the streets, the prouder.
We laughed at the bright clothes of a prostitute,
a man sitting on a curb with a bottle in his hand.
We smelled barbecue cooking in dented washtubs,
      and our mouths watered.
As much as we wanted it we couldn't take the chance.

Rhythm and blues came from the windows, the throaty voice of
      a woman lost in the bass, in the drums, in the dirty down
      and out, the grind.
"I love to see a funeral, then I know it ain't mine."
We rolled our windows down so that the waves rolled over us
      like blood.
We hoped to pass invisible, knowing on Monday we would
      return safely to our jobs, the post office and classroom.
We wanted our sufferings to be offered up as tender meat,
and our triumphs to be belted out in raucous song.
We had lost our voice in the suburbs, in Conant Gardens,
      where each brick house delineated a fence of silence;
we had lost the right to sing in the street and damn creation.

We returned to wash our hairdo of them,
to smell them
whose very existence
tore us down to the human.

Natasha Trethewey

Saturday Matinee

When I first see *Imitation of Life*,
the 1959 version with Lana Turner
and Sandra Dee, I already know the story
has a mixed girl in it—someone like me,
a character I can shape my life to.
It begins with a still of blue satin
upon which diamonds fall, slowly at first,
and then faster, crowding my television
with rays of light, a sparkling world.

In my room I'm a Hollywood starlet
stretched across my bed, beneath
a gold and antique white canopy,
heavy swags cut from fringed brocade
and pieced together—all remnants
of my grandmother's last job.
Down the hall, my mother whispers
resistance, my stepfather's voice louder
than the static of an old seventy-eight.

Lana Turner glides on screen,
the camera finding her in glowing white,
golden-haired among the crowd.
She is not like my mother, or
the mixed girl's mother—that tired black maid
she hires—and I can see why the mixed girl
wants her, instead, a mother always smiling
from a fifties magazine. She doesn't want
the run-down mama, her blues—

dark circles around the eyes,
that weary step and *hush-baby* tone.
My gold room is another world.
I turn the volume up, over the dull smack,
the stumbling for balance, the clutter of voices
in the next room. I'll be Sandra Dee,
and Lana Turner, my mother—our lives
an empty screen, pale blue, diamonds falling
until it's all covered up.

Alan Shapiro

The Fight

1969

The black girl next to me was cheering under her breath
As the two girls, white and black, appeared to freeze

Together for a moment with their hands locked
In each other's hair before they toppled over

In a blur of pummeling. Get the bitch, Dolores,
She was saying, abuse her, cat her up, her faint voice

Giddily enraged, yet cautious too, confused,
It almost seemed, uncertain of its own excitement,

As if she'd grown so used to wishing for what she saw
She only half-believed she saw it now before her.

Right on, girl, right on, she cheered a little louder,
The voice rousing itself past hesitation or demurral.

And though the rest of us stood there, dumbly looking on,
And would later try hard to range in, cage what we saw

With outrage, stories, rumors of who said what and why,
Till we could think it didn't have to do with us,

My friends and I—white friends and black friends—
Did any of us at the time make any move to stop it?

Wasn't hers the only voice of what we all were feeling,
And were dismayed to feel, were too well trained to show?

All of us rapt by the tribal solvent of our civil dream,
By the frenzy of slashing nails, ripped blouses, shrieks

And muffled groans; the girls dissolving in the mouth
Of rage beyond their names, or *sex*, or even the history

That carefully prepared them for the dissolution—
Dissolving in the idiot mouth till in the teeth of it

They could only go on tearing at each other, kicking
And scratching even after the teacher intervened.

Patricia Smith

Ain't But One Way Heaven Makes Sense
Or, Annie Pearl Smith Explains the U.S.
Space Program

First of all, y'all fools. See what's right in front of you,
then got folks telling you ain't seeing what you
just saw, other folks saying you saw more than you did.
Heaven is where my Jesus live. Just one way to get there,
no great big shiny ship can rise up on that sacred. They think
they gon' look the Lord dead in his eye, asking questions
with nerve enough to wait for answers? No man gon' reach
down, just scoop up moon, even if Mr. Cronkite say he did.
Them white men way out in a desert somewhere, stumbling
round in them blowed-up suits with movie stuff back a' them,
laughing inside those glass heads. And colored folks *aahing*
and *oohing* like the number's in and they got money comin.'
Chile, I sho' didn't raise you to be this much fool this fast.
People got to pray they way up. One small step ain't enough.

Ana Castillo

Dirty Mexican

"Dirty Mexican, dirty, dirty Mexican!"
And i said, "i'll kick your ass, Dago bitch!"
tall for my race, strutted right past
black projects,
leather jacket, something sharp
in my pocket
to Pompeii School,
Get those Dago girls with teased-up hair
and Cadillacs,
Mafia-bought clothes,
sucking on summer Italian lemonades.
Boys with Sicilian curls got high
at Sheridan Park, mutilated a prostitute one night.
i scrawled in chalk all over sidewalks
MEXICAN POWER CON/SAFOS
crashed their dances,
get them broads, corner 'em in the bathroom,
in the hallway, and their loudmouthed mamas
calling from the windows: "Roxanne!" "Antoinette!"
And when my height wouldn't do
my mouth called their bluff:
"That's right, honey, I'm a Mexican!
Watchu gonna do about it?" Since they didn't
Want their hair or lipstick mussed they
Shrugged their shoulders 'til distance gave way:
"Dirty Mexican, dirty Mexican bitch."
Made me look back, right up their faces,
"Watchu say?" And it started all over again.

Patricia Smith

Asking for a Heart Attack

For Aretha Franklin

Aretha. Deep butter dipped, scorched pot liquor,
swift lick off the sugar cane. Vaselined knees
clack gospel, hinder the waddling South. 'Retha.
Greased, she glows in limelit circle, defending
her presence with a sanctified moan, ass rumbling
toward curfew's backstreets where jukes still gulp silver.

Goddess of Hoppin' John and bumped buttermilk,
girl know Jesus by His *first* name. She the one
sang His drooping down from ragged wooden T,
dressed Him in blood-red shine, conked that holy head,
rustled up excuses for bus fare and took
the Deity downtown. They found a neon
backslap, coaxed the DJ and slid electric
till the lights slammed on. *Don't know where you goin',
who you going with, but you sho can't stay here.*

Aretha taught the Good Son slow, dirty
words for His daddy's handiwork, laughed as he
first sniffed whiskey's surface, hissed him away when
he sought to touch His hand to the blue in her.
She was young then, spindly and thin ribs paining,
her heartbox thrumming in a suspicious key.
So Jesus blessed her, opened her throat and taught
her to *wail that way she do, Lawd she do wail
that way don't she do that wail the way she do
wail that way, don't she? That girl can wail that way.*

Now when Aretha's fleeing screech jump from juke
and reach been-done-wrong bone, all the Lord can do
is stand at a wary distance and applaud.
Oh yeah, and maybe shield His heart a little.

So you question her several shoulders,
the soft stairs of flesh leading to her chins,
the steel bones of an impossible dress
gnawing raw into bubbling obliques?

Ain't your mama never schooled you in how
black women collect the world, build other
bodies onto our own? No earthly man
knows the solution to our hips, asses
urgent as sirens, our titties bursting
with traveled roads. Ask Aretha just what
Jesus whispered to her that night about
the gospel hidden in lard and sugar.
She'll tell you why black girls grow fat
away from the world, and toward each other.

Kate Daniels

Late Apology to Doris Haskins

Come in, lone black girl, and sit among us.
And if there are twenty of us and only
one of you? No matter. New laws say
it must be so, and that we should
ignore the inequality that clouds
our visions of each other.

                    And so—
we sit here through the dragging day,
clock hands lagging maddeningly,
lessons sidelined, watching you
not watching us—your head
with its plethora of plastic barrettes,
your neat white socks creaming
your ankles. We circle you, sniffing.
No one dares to enter the restroom
after you, perchance to occupy
the cool white seat you might have sat
upon for brief relief. And not one
of us will march beside you to the lunchroom
or the asphalt field where we play our games.
Each day we hope the threats of bombs your presence
summons to what used to be our all-white school
will come again. For hours, then, we'll be out of class,
and free to wallow on the green front lawn, ignoring you
sitting off to the side, alone as usual, your plaid-skirted lap
filled with the torn-up blooms of buttercups.

We don't know why you are among us, or what
your presence means, or why we must attend
the mystery you make—a little girl who's more or less
identical to us despite the tales our parents tell.
Evenings, we watch them demonstrating on tv
in long, hot lines outside the board of education.
We read their signs and memorize the close-ups
of their faces twisted up in hate.
We watch them, as we eat our meals
on trays before the screen.

                             Your family
must watch them, too, before they kill the set
and send you off to bathe and pray and sleep.
Perhaps your mother stands, like mine,
late into the night, pressing flat the wrinkles
in your skirt with a hot iron, her mind
crowded with old terror she no longer
has the energy to fight. In the morning,
she will send her only daughter—a girl of ten—
forward into new light to vanquish it at last.
As will mine send forth *her* only daughter
to face the other side of your mother's terror.
And we will sit beside each other, Doris, gleaming
in our brand new classroom, sanctioned by law,
spelling unfamiliar words, and calculating
complicated sums.

Sybil Estess

In My Alice Blue Gown

(Poplarville, Mississippi, April, 1959)

I see the blood
after our late-night April prom:
red puddles on white-marble steps.
I'm sixteen—

I'm the soprano who sings
myriad romantic solos
with the prom-night band.
They say he raped her—

a white woman. They can't
take a chance on random justice,
with daughters, wives,
secretaries to protect. . . .

The elected deputy sheriff
lays the jail-key on his desk
beside the courthouse's open windows,
where the jail is on the top floor.

The deputy rushes with the mob
into the cell and yells for no one
to notice or tell. Nobody does
but one female witness

who later blows her brains out.

But I already know—oh yes:
the world isn't good. And white
isn't white and black merely black.

My world's all color, counted
by chance. I'm white. Mack Parker's black
and it's Mississippi, 1959.
In high school next year

I'll be a senior.
Someday I'll leave Poplarville.
The cloudy world is open
 but oh so scary:

I sing "In My Alice Blue Gown,"
a thirties' tune. What time is this,
and what red space must I run from—
to flee far enough away from here?

Rebecca Balcárcel

Ave America

Plenty of corn, no tortillas:
Iowa 1968,
and only her eyes—my Peace Corps girl
speak my flamenco, my Latino
hers the only heat slicing
through snowstorm, starestorm,
blue eyes and blond hair storm
and, hombre, it's November and zero degrees
when walk off the plane into marriage, into the GED.
I swing a night-school-English machete
until I'm a Bachelor of Arts *cum laude,*
and why not Husband, I'm thinking,
why not Lover, *Novio,* French Kisser,
why not Tender Toucher of Arts,
why not Heartbeat, Drumbeat, Got-the-beat
Man or Woman, certified.
Plenty of corn; at last tortillas:
flat as social security cards,
circular as compass on-the-dough,
no woman's hand, no grandma's pan,
fat packages side-by-side, airtight with twist-tie
cornmeal abacus in the deep freeze.
My mother writes, what is America?
Is dancing the alarm-clocked sunrise,
dancing *fútbol* turned soccer
dancing taco turned Bell.
I ballroom to classroom, teach the Tango,
the lingo, the trying-hard gringo,

the school-teacher trot, chase-the-mortgage chacha
dance for *mí familia,*
dance for my life.

Tim Seibles

Allison Wolff

Like a river at night, her hair—
the sky starless, streetlights
glossing the full dark of it:
Was she Jewish? I was seventeen,

an "Afro-American" senior
transferred to a suburban school
that held just a few of us.
And she had light-brown eyes

and tight tube tops   and skin
white enough to read by
in a dim room. It was impossible
not to be curious.

Me and my boy, Terry, talked about
"pink babes" sometimes: we watched
I Dream of Jeannie and could see Barbara
Eden—in her skimpy finery—lounging

on our very own lonely sofas.
We wondered what white girls were
really like, as if they'd been raised
by the freckled light of the moon.

I can't remember Allison's voice
but the loud tap of her strapless heels
clacking down the halls is still clear.
Autumn, 1972: Race was the elephant

sitting on everybody. Even
as a teenager, I took the weight
as part of the weather, a sort of heavy
humidity felt inside and in the streets.

One day, *once upon a time*, she laughed
with me in the cafeteria—something
about the Tater Tots, I guess,
or the electric-blue Jell-O. Usually,

it was just some of us displaced brothers
talkin' noise, actin' crazy, so she
caught all of us way off-guard. Then,
after school, I waved   and she smiled

and the sun was out—that 3 o'clock,
after-school sun rubbing the sidewalk
with the shadows of trees—

and while the wind pitched the last
of September, we started talking
and the dry leaves shook and sizzled.

In so many ways, I was still a child,
though I wore my seventeen years
like a matador's cape.

The monsters that murdered
Emmett Till—were they everywhere?
I didn't know. I didn't know enough
to worry enough about the story
white people kept trying to tell.

And, given the thing that American is,
maybe sometimes such stupidity works
for the good. Occasionally,

History offers a reprieve, everything
leading up to a particular moment
suddenly declared a mistrial:
so I'm a black boy suddenly

walking the Jenkintown streets
with a white girl—so ridiculously
conspicuous   we must've been
invisible. I remember her mother

not being home and cold Coca Cola
in plastic cups and the delicious
length of Allison's tongue   and
we knew, without saying anything
we were kissing the *color line*

goodbye   and on and on for an hour
we kissed, hardly breathing, the light almost
blinding whenever we unclosed our eyes—
as if we had discovered the dreaming door
to a different country   and were walking

out   as if we *could* actually
walk the glare we'd been
born into: as if my hand
on her knee, her hand
on my hand, my hand
in her hair, her mouth
on my mouth opened
and opened and opened

Danny Romero

This Day

Two of my older brothers
atop the wooden pallets in the backyard
stacked four feet off the ground
beneath the waning sun

They each wear a glove
black leather on a fist
held up in the air
high above their bowed heads

like Tommie Smith and John Carlos
at the Olympic Games in Mexico City
on KABC Channel 7 Wide World of Sports
the day before

We live in an old Mexican neighborhood
surrounded on three sides
by the larger black community
and this day it feels really good

Lorenzo Thomas

Back in the Day

When we were boys
We called each other "Man"
With a long *n*
Pronounced as if a promise

We wore felt hats
That took a month to buy
In small installments
Shiny Florsheim or Stacy Adams shoes
Carried our dancing gait
And flashed our challenge

Breathing our aspirations into words
We harmonized our yearnings to the night
And when old folks on porches dared complain
We cussed them out
   under our breaths
And walked away
    And once a block away
Held learned speculations
About the character of their relations
With their mothers

It's true
That every now and then
We killed each other
Borrowed a stranger's car

Burned down a house
But most boys went to jail
For knocking up a girl
He really   truly   deeply   loved
        really   truly   deeply

But was too young
Too stupid, poor, or scared
To marry

Since then I've learned
Some things don't never change:

The breakfast chatter of the newly met
Our disappointment

With the world as given

Today,

News and amusements
Filled with automatic fire
Misspelled alarms
Sullen posturings and bellowed anthems
Our scholars say
Young people doubt tomorrow

This afternoon I watched
A group of young men
Or tall boys
Handsome and shining with the strength of futures
Africa's stubborn present
To a declining white man's land
Lamenting

As boys always did and do
Time be moving on
Some things don't never change
And how

      back in the day
Well
      things were somehow better

They laughed and jived
Slapped hands
And called each other "Dog"

V.

WAR PHOTOGRAPHS

there's a man with a gun over there

Robert Bly

At a March Against the Vietnam War:

Washington, November 27, 1965

Newspapers rise high in the air over Maryland.

We walk about, bundles in coats
And sweaters in the late November sun.

Looking down, I see feet moving
Calmly, gaily,
Almost as if separated from their bodies.

But there is something moving in the dark somewhere
Just beyond
The edge of our eyes: a boat
Covered with machine guns
Moving along under trees.

It is the darkness among pine trees
That the Puritans brushed
As they went out to kill turkeys.
At the edge of the jungle clearing
The Puritan darkness explodes
On the ground.

We have carried around this cup of darkness.

We have longed to pour it over our heads.

We make war as if it were a sacrament.

Chana Bloch

The Spoils

The mother of Sisera cried through the lattice,
Why is his chariot so long in coming?

Judges 5:28

An Israeli soldier, just back from the '67 war,
gave me a photo he found of a mother and son,
a talisman the enemy wore to battle
in his khaki shirt pocket.

What was he was offering me that day
—a trophy? a souvenir?
I didn't ask and he answered:
All he wanted was to get home safe.

His mother, my neighbor, fought the war
cigarette by cigarette
in a Jerusalem shelter,
clinging to the phone like Sisera's mother.

Home safe, he let me take
a shot of him holding his dazed mother,
a shot of him cradling his gun.

Then he gave me the photo he found
in a dead man's pocket
and without thinking I took that too.

Kate Daniels

War Photograph

A naked child is running
along the path toward us,
her arms stretched out,
her mouth open,
the world turned to trash
behind her.

She is running from the smoke
and the soldiers, from the bodies
of her mother and little sister
thrown down into a ditch,
from the blown-up bamboo hut
from the melted pots and pans.
And she is also running from the gods
who have changed the sky to fire
and puddled the earth with skin and blood.
She is running—my god—to us,
10,000 miles away,
reading the caption
beneath her picture
in a weekly magazine.
All over the country
we're feeling sorry for her
and being appalled at the war
being fought in the other world.
She keeps on running, you know,
after the shutter of the camera
clicks. She's running to us.

For how can she know,
her feet beating a path
on another continent?
How can she know
what we really are?
From the distance, we look
so terribly human.

Tess Gallagher

Sugarcane

Some nights go on in an afterwards so secure
they don't need us, though sometimes one exactly
corresponds to its own powers of elemental tirelessness.
A prodigious heaviness comes over it that upswings it
into taking us, like the seizure knowing is,
back into its mouth. One blue-violet night in Hawaii during
the Vietnam War pinions me against

the war's prolonged foreboding as I relive it yet
in the preposterous homecoming the generals arranged
for their men on R & R in that meant-to-be paradise. Wives
flown in to bungalows and beach-side hotels, their suitcases
crammed with department-store negligees for conjugal trysts
that seem pornographic now in their psycho-erotic
rejuvenation of the killing. But he

was my husband. And I was glad he hadn't gone down
in a craze of flak in some widow-maker out of Da Nang
zigzagging over to Cambodia to drop its load. Glad
my government had a positive view of sexual continuity,
wanted its men in loving arms at their war's halftime.
We would meet, as some would not. Seven months gone—
daily letters, tapes and that telepathic hotline reserved
for saints and gods, except when women's wartime
solicitations to their mates usurp all tidy elevations.
But what did

those heavenly bodies, those angel currents, make of so much
heavy panting and suppositional boudoir?

Or of homeward-yanking fantasies interspersed
with napalm, sniper fire, firebombing, mines—the dead,
the wounded lifted out by helicopter?
I would see you in and out of khaki
again. Was early to the island, tanning a luxurious khaki
into my sallow in a luminescent bikini after months
working the dawn shift on a medical ward.
But the night is tired of its history
and doesn't know how we got here. Children

are what it wants. Though we didn't know it, no amount of
innocent gladness of the young to meet again on earth
would bring them back. Nor could they be revived
in the glower of long rain-shattered afternoons as we labored
to push ourselves back into each other.
They were gone from us, those children.
As if disenfranchisements like this were some mercurial,
unvoiceable by-product of the country's mania, its payment
in kind for those flaming children

we took into the elsewhere. There was so much to spare you
I had to overuse loving as balm, a cauterizing
forgetfulness to prise you to me. Maybe the exuberance
of our stretching all the way to first-love, that *always*
to each other, allowed our lack its comfortless posture,
and we were given respite in which a quiet light
thought us human enough to slough off its breath-saddened
anguish. And then I saw you

made new again in moonlight. Not as yourself, but as
more entirely made of pain in its power
of always usurping what might also
be true. As I was true in moonlight, preparing to meet you,
lifted by the raw gaiety of my brother's shipmates
taking shore leave the night before you touched down,

the gleeful carload of us emptied into a field
because I'd never tasted sugarcane.
Breaking off the chalky stalks,

my juiceless sucking and licking the woody fiber
in darkness, the flat way it discarded me, as if another, greedier
mouth had been there first. Then the young man's voice,
my hand with his around it lifted, so he tore with his biting
the stalk I held, squeezing my hand until the full pressure
of his jaw passed into me
as what was needed for sweetness to yield.

And since sweet pressure is all I gave—that boy's
unguarded kiss in moonlight was yours, was any god's invitation
to how we'd meant our love to close us,
close, in a little rest, allowing
that sweet scythe of unfoulable kindred tenderness, before
the rest. That biting down on us.
The heavy pressure that demands its sweetness as it mouths
and sucks, until it finds us with its love-letting teeth.

H. Palmer Hall

This Poem

This poem is not about Vietnam or war.
It is not about the Central Highlands:
that place where three countries touch
and where blood spilled over a small hill
and nothing lived save through chance.

This poem is about love in a time
when love could no longer bloom,
about affection and what we might call
grace in a time when grace had fled
to some other land, to some other time

This poem contains lotus blossoms
and tigers in dense jungles and elephants
and mountains and streams without end
and villages and paddies filled with water
and two people embracing behind bamboo

stands. This poem is about soft passion
in the midst or drenching rains, small fires
and empty houses. It contains no free fire
zones or carpet bombing. Only, sometimes,
a hint of passing currents, of raw nothing.

H. Palmer Hall

We Have Seen the Enemy

Eddie Adams resented the use
of his most famous photograph:
a captured VC, Genera Loan.
We see masses of brain tissue,

shattered bone flying out.
The prisoner's shirt stretches
across his chest and stomach:
checked cloth against a cityscape.

Other pictures command our attention
though not so well: a young VC prisoner,
bayonet dragged sharply against his neck.
Adams notes: he talked. An ARVN

pushes a spearhead against a VC's neck,
skin dimpled in. He, too, talked. ARVN Captain,
fist clenched, the prisoner reels from the blow
to his face, staggered. No commentary.

H. Palmer Hall

Father Buddha

I walked two klicks down Le Loi Street
to a schoolyard, a Buddha broken in the dust
shattered by a rocket meant for us,
and saw you sitting in his hand
tossing carved pieces of the statue's feet,
not even caring where they'd land.

What mattered was that I did not want to be
where and what I was and saw
that you had also had no choice. Some law,
legal in my case, chance in yours,
with no way out that you or I could see,
gave me a twelve month, you a lifetime, tour.

We shared a cigarette and watched the smoke
rise into the red dust Pleiku air.
You laughed, blew smoke rings with the flair
that comes only when you're very young.
You told me I was on the Buddha's throat
and should beware the Buddha's tongue.

I remember that once, when the war was calm,
we laughed and played with shattered stones,
and know there can be no way to atone
for all the wounds, the pain, the death.
If you still live, rest quietly in father Buddha's palm:
if not, sleep peacefully in the Buddha's breath.

Judith Arcana

Correspondence

The first cards had pictures:
Kodachrome. Vistaview
birds on mountains
flowers on walls
flying and climbing
in countries I'd never seen.

The early letters came
in thick blue envelopes
franked with bright stamps:
queens, castles
monuments with flags
rising, waving over graves.

Later a card said Honey
I've got to rush, we're moving
but I thought you
would like this: scenery
lonely that way you love.
Gulls fly inland here for miles.

Later letters said Jesus
I can't believe what's happening
here. I mean: I don't
want to. You should believe
I'll come back, believe
so I will, like a fairy tale.

Cards stopped. Letters
came in thin brown sleeves
saying: How can I tell you
What can I say and When
will we understand how to
do this, how not to do this?

No tellers. Long time.
Radio, tv, movies
newspapers. magazines.
I wrote: I was

answering carefully
what you might have sent.

Then the ones with cuts:
blacked-out phrases
written on transparent tissue
haphazardly folded,
jammed into white
bag-like covers.

No stamps: only
the government postmark.

Edward Hirsch

The Lottery

Hundreds of us pressed tightly together
In the south lounge of the Forum
To watch the lottery on a giant TV screen.

We were stuck in the heart of the country,
But in Washington, the men in sober suits
Stood together on the bright stage

And faced the rolling cameras
For the invocation blessing our country,
Which would be a blessing to the world,

And the roll call of birth dates.
The mood among our motley seemed
Festive and fearful, seething, curious.

The selection: a random sequence
Of blue capsules mixed in a shoe box
And pulled out of a glass bowl.

September 14ᵗʰ was the first date
Pasted onto an enormous white board
With 365 more empty slots.

April 24ᵗʰ: the lucky second.
Someone muttered, "*I'm fucked*";
Someone lit a joint, as at a concert;

And the girl next to me began to sob
For her high-school boyfriend in Cedar Falls
Whose birthday was *December 30th*.

History existed only in textbooks,
But it arrived for us on December 1st, 1969,
With the Selective Service System.

Those blue plastic capsules opened,
And people drifted away when their days
Were called to call their parents

Or get drunk or pack for Saskatchewan—
Where *was* it, anyway?—or muse over
The randomness of dying in Vietnam.

David Huddle

Nerves

Training I received did not apply
because Cu Chi District was not Fort Jackson.
Funniest thing, they had dogs like any-
where, used them for sandwich meat, I ate one
once, but I guess you want to know if I
ever shot somebody—didn't—would have—
curious about it, but my job gave
one duty, to ask questions. I'd lie

if I said some weren't women, children,
old men; I'd lie too if I claimed these
memories weren't part of my life, but then
shame is natural, wear it, every day
think of bursting from sleep when mortars dropped:
crazy run to a dark hole, damp sandbags.

David Huddle

Them

Sergeant Dieu, frail Vietnamese man,
once sat down with me, shirtless, on my bunk
and most astonishingly in my opinion
(not his) squeezed a pimple on my back.
My first trip to the field, I saw Vietnamese
infantry troops, loaded with combat gear,
walking the paddy dikes and holding hands.
I was new then. I thought they were queer.

Co Ngoc at the California Laundry
wouldn't say any of our words, but she
explained anyway a Vietnamese treatment
for sore throat: over where it's sore inside
you rub outside until that hurts too. That
way won't work for American pain. I've tried.

David Huddle

Work

I am a white, Episcopal-raised, almost
college-educated, North American male.
Sergeant Tri, my interpreter, is engrossed
in questioning our detainee, a small,
bad-smelling man in rags who claims to be
a farmer. I am filling the blanks
of a form, writing down what Sergeant Tri
tells me. This is dull. Suddenly Tri yanks

our detainee to his feet, slaps him twice
across the bridge of his nose. The farmer
whimpers. Tri says the farmer has lied and waits
for orders. Where I grew up my father
waits at the door while my mother finishes
packing his lunch. I must tell Tri what next.

David Jauss

The Border

The morning sun slants
        through the kitchen window
as I drink my coffee and listen

to Miles answer the birdsong
        in the evergreens.
It's easy, sitting in the light

of a day not yet spoiled by failure,
        to forget the country half a world
and half a life away, where night

is just beginning, the sky
        over the Mekong River
bruised black as the border on a map,

dividing the world into darkness
        and light, the two
countries we're all citizens of.

But by the time I come home from work
        the border has crept up the yard
toward the hedge of honeysuckle

and I sit in a lawn chair at the edge
        of the shrunken light,
drink sweating in my hand, and brood

over the lie I told at lunch, the wrong
        I did a friend, the right gesture
that was too late to do anything

but hurt—all the petty failures
        of an average day—
until, for comfort, I call up

the larger shame that soldier felt,
        when I was him,
to see the light leaving

the eyes of the dead. I remind myself
        I have killed no one
today. But still the sky

darkens like a map drawn
        and redrawn on the same
soiled paper, each gradation

of darkness a further border,
        complicating location
and fear. To play music now

would be one more betrayal
        so I sit in a silence made larger
by the cry of crickets. Then

the light is gone
        and I'm in that other country
where nothing is clear, where the border

is everywhere.

Michael Anania

A Second-Hand Elegy

for Douglas Dickey, Pfc. U.S.M.C.

"How can I be bitter?"
 the fence-rows rolling with the land;
the last full measure of Ohio
measured by fence-rows compressing,
though parallel above receding hills,
the mixed hues of damp Spring greenery.

"I never knew him to be angry or afraid."
that is, assured of providence
moving within the accidental turnings
of his life, he moved with certainty
among the farmyard's familiar disorders
and occasionally outward toward Dayton.

"He glanced for an instant at his friends—
        for only an instant—and then he jumped."
riding through Dayton on Saturday night
making the rounds, block by block,
the car radio marking time—
Downtown   Downtown—
the evening blush of neon blooming.
into damp city air, the blue
clarity of mercury-lamp arcades;
four of them slouched in a Chevrolet
exhaust the evening, waiting for something to happen.

Note: In April of 1968 Douglas Dickey was awarded the Congressional Medal of Honor posthumously for throwing himself on a hand grenade during an engagement with the enemy in Viet Nam.

Yusef Komunyakaa

Communique

Bob Hope's on stage, but we want the Gold Diggers,
want a flash of legs

through the hemorrhage of vermilion, giving us
something to kill for.

We want our hearts wrung out like rags & ground down
to Georgia dust

while Cobras drag the perimeter, gliding along the sea,
swinging searchlights

through the trees. The assault & battery of hot pink
glitter erupts

as the rock 'n' roll band tears down the night—caught
in a safety net

of brightness, The Gold Diggers convulse. White legs
shimmer like strobes.

The lead guitarist's right foot's welded to his wah-wah.
"I thought you said

Aretha was gonna be here?" "Man, I don't wanna see
no Miss America."

"There's Lola." The sky is blurred by magnesium flares
over the fishing boats.

"Shit, man, she looks awful white to me." We duck
when we hear the quick

metallic hiss of the mountain of amplifiers struck by
a flash of rain.

After the show's packed up & gone, after the choppers
have flown out backwards,

after the music & colors have died slowly in our heads,
& the downpour's picked up,

we sit holding our helmets like rain-polished skulls.

Yusef Komunyakaa

Tu Do Sheet

Music divides the evening.
I close my eyes & can see
men drawing lines in the dust.
America pushes through the membrane
of mist & smoke, & I'm a small boy
again in Bogalusa. *White Only*
signs & Hank Snow. But tonight
I walk into a place where bar girls
fade like tropical birds. When
I order a beer, the mama-san
behind the counter acts as if she
can't understand, while her eyes
skirt each white face, as Hank Williams
calls from the psychedelic jukebox.
We have played Judas where
only machine-gun fire brings us
together. Down the street
black GIs hold to their turf also.
An off-limits sign pulls me
deeper into alleys, as I look
for a softness behind these voices
wounded by their beauty & war.
Back in the bush at Dak To
& Khe Sanh, we fought
the brothers of these women
we now run to hold in our arms.
There's more than a nation
inside us, as black & white

soldiers touch the same lovers
minutes apart, tasting
each other's breath,
without knowing these rooms
run into each other like tunnels
leading to the underworld.

Yusef Komunyakaa

Hanoi Hannah

Ray Charles! His voice
calls from waist-high grass,
& we duck behind gray sandbags.
"Hello, Soul Brothers. Yeah,
Georgia's also on my mind."
Flares bloom over the trees.
"Here's Hannah again.
Let's see if we can't
light her goddamn fuse
this time." Artillery
shells carve a white arc
against dusk. Her voice rises
from a hedgerow on our left.
"It's Saturday night in the States.
Guess what your woman's doing tonight.
I think I'll let Tina Turner
tell you, you homesick GIs."
Howitzers buck like a herd
of horses behind concertina.
"You know you're dead men,
don't you? You're dead
as King today in Memphis.
Boys, you're surrounded by
General Tran Do's division."
Her knife-edge song cuts
deep as a sniper's bullet.
"Soul Brothers, what you dying for?"

We lay down a white-klieg
trail of tracers. Phantom jets
fan out over the trees.
Artillery fire zeros in.
Her voice grows flesh
& we can see her falling
into words, a bleeding flower
no one knows the true name for.
"You're lousy shots, GIs."
Her laughter floats up
as though the airways are
buried under our feet.

Alicia Ostriker

VOX POPULI

The people, yes...
> —Carl Sandburg

The people, yes, are the poets. Let me make that clear.
A soldier's talk being, you see,
brisker than yours or mine, naturally
brings things, as it were, to a head:
"Kilroy was here"
with his curious nose looking flip
all over Europe,
or what the G. I. said
to the *Times* man in the Asian jungle,
employing the nickname game
of primitive art, whereby *Viet Cong*
is *Victor Charlie*, or politely *Charles,*
to wit a symbol—because those
yellow folks inside the flames
may easily be grandmothers or infant girls.
Not men at all—with sensuous imagery
for a true, direct, and vivid statement:
"I love the smell of Charlie burning."
We see how clear a thing
language becomes here, and are perforce content:
the line is poetry. Poets, remember this,
"I love it," he added for rhetorical emphasis.

Stanley Plumly

The Day of the Failure in Saigon,
Thousands in the Streets,
Hundreds Killed, A Lucky Few
Hanging On the Runners of Evacuating Copters

Old arguments among old arguments
about the common species, late into the night,
nineteen sixty eight, give or take a year,
give or take uncivil disobedience,
cities terrorized, the assassin honing in,
and the example still in front of us
the draft and Vietnam, with the evening
TV Cronkite, the generals' guarantees,
the lottery of dead, the Johnson/Nixon
death mask filling up the screen,
villages destroyed like magic with a match,
a naked burning girl no bigger than a stick
running toward the camera, a man, Viet
Cong, looking at the lens, his face already
oatmeal, while here, on the other side
of the pictures, all two hundred of our human
bones intact, the vestiges, appendages
in place, the Jacob's ladder following
the spine, the warm brain within the cold
brain—or reverse, reptilian, mammalian—
traces of the graduating faunae and their gods
lingering inside us yet alien as children,
and there's a bird, a kind of bird,
alive in there, too, between the raptor
and the wren, of a size we can't imagine,

soaring in the thermals or secret in the hedge
speaking in the bird-talk we call singing,
a missing link along the chain of being,

Patricia Smith

Minus One, Minus One More

Carol Burnett tugs an ear, waves toodly-doo to the camera eye.
It's ten o'clock, and a white mechanized man asked if I, a child,
know where my children are. No, but it's time for the news, time
for the insisting war, and the preposterous Philco—half monster
TV screen, half bulky, functional phonograph—blares jungle, its
flat glass face filled with streaked pans of crushed foliage, the whir
of blades, dust-dreary GIs heaving through quick-slamming throats.
Lurching toward the ledges of copters, they screech commands,
instructions, prayers, struggle to cram blooded lumps back into
their uniforms—*dead there, there, let's see, almost dead over there*—
a hand dangling by tendrils, a left eye imploded, black-and-white
red etches slow roadways into the back of a dimming hand. Beneath
the lack of hue, a white buzz, a lazy scroll of dates and numbers:
This is how many gone today, how many last week, last month,
this year. Big Daddy Cronkite's eyes glaze, consider closing, refocus.

Think of all the children plopped in front of this unscripted boom
to pass the time. Think of Tom turning Jerry's head into spectacular
dust, then this, our first official war smashing into the family room,
blurring into cinema, into lesson. It's how we learned to subtract.

Katherine Solomon

Expatriates, 1967

How could we guess there would be no cherries
in Canada that year when blossoms
covered our tree like a bride's veil?
But the green fruit withered, turned
to dry brown bangles and drooped
in the summer branches like old medals. Sick

of kissing boys goodbye, we'd packed our van,
turned our backs on Boston, and headed over
the Peace Bridge. We stopped when we saw
that little house for rent, moored
to the tree like a boxy boat, afloat
on the Scarborough wind in a country not at war.

On the sun porch we set up our sewing machines,
made fringed leather vests for draft-dodgers,
wore bell bottoms and tie-dyed tee-shirts, no bras.
We'd wave to the neighborhood women, granny grackles
in black shawls and stockings, and they would waggle
their mother-fingers back at us, calling
from the sidewalk in Italian or Portuguese.
We thought they must be telling us to put on shoes
or comb our hair—but it wasn't very long
before a truant officer stopped by. He laughed
to see our ages on American driver's licenses.
To the old, he said, *everyone young
looks illegal.* Because we were playing

at angels-of-mercy, we took in a friend's
friend from California, a blond all-American
Army deserter, never dreaming he liked to shoot
up, until the cold night we found him slumped
in a green vinyl chair against the kitchen wall, needle
hanging like a glass leech from the top of his foot.
He might have burned our house down
if his cigarette hadn't landed in the bowl
of red jello and CoolWhip wilting on the table.

Not even coffee spooned into his drooling mouth,
or ice cubes dumped down his skinny chest
could rouse him, so we slapped him around a little—
and it felt good. We pulled socks and shoes
on his clammy feet, and walked him
around the block a dozen times. He begged
to go inside, so we took him to a diner
for more coffee, and played his favorite song—
Brown-Eyed Girl, C-4 on the jukebox—
until we ran out of change.

While he ate, I held the pale hair at his nape
in my fist to keep his face from falling
flat into the French fries and gravy on his plate,
and Niki told the waitress that he always got sick—
sometimes even fainted—the night before
he tried out for a part.

After three cups of coffee, he started to cry,
then turned away, knees stuck out into the aisle,
clasped hands dragging down between them like an anchor.
We told him everything would be all right, patted
his back, promised not to send him back to Uncle Sam
to break apart in jail, or get sent to Vietnam.

We told him he didn't have to kill anyone. *Who says
I don't want to kill no one, huh?* He wiped his nose
on the back of his hand. *Just don't want to die is all.*

When we finally steered him out the door at three a.m.,
a baby whore in a hot-pink leather miniskirt
and nylon baseball jacket—*Mississauga*—
followed us, singing *Who Killed Liberty Valance?*
all the way to our bungalow-lined side street,
where guardian angels in long black shawls and nightgowns
peered from shadows, white hair flapping at the night.
Early apples, touched too by some blight, fell
around us, victim to another order of war.
They stickied up the sidewalk, made us pick
our way home like three drunk sailors
searching for a friendly ship.

Alicia Ostriker

Cambodia

My son Gabriel was born on May 14, 1970, during the
Vietnam War, a few days after the United States invaded
Cambodia, and a few days after four students had been
shot by National Guardsmen at Kent State University in
Ohio during a protest demonstration.

On May 1, President Nixon announced Operation Total
Victory, sending 5,000 American troops into Cambodia
to destroy North Vietnamese military sanctuaries, in a
test of "our will and character," so that America would not
seem "a pitiful helpless giant" or "accept the first defeat in
its proud 190-year history."
He wanted his own war.

> The boy students stand in line
> at Ohio State
> each faces a Guardsman in gasmask
> each a bayonet point at his throat.

U.S. air cavalry thrusts into Kompong Chain province,
seeking bunkers. Helicopters descend on "The Parrot's
Beak." B-52's heavily bomb Red sanctuaries. Body count!
Body count high! in the hundreds. The President has
explained, and explains again, that this is not an invasion.

Monday, May 4th, at Kent State, laughing demonstrators
and rock-throwers on a lawn spotted with dandelions.
It was after a weekend of beerdrinking. Outnumbered
Guardsmen, partially encircled and out of tear gas, begin

to retreat uphill, turn, kneel, in unison aim their guns. Four students lie dead, seventeen wounded. 441 colleges and universities strike, many shut down.

The President says: "When dissent turns to violence, it invites tragedy."

A veteran of the Khe Sanh says: "I saw enough violence, blood and death and I vowed never again, never again . . . Now I must protest. I'm not a leftist but I can't go any further. I'll do damn near anything to stop the war now."

A man in workclothes tries to seize an American flag from a student. "That's my flag! I fought for it! You have no right to it! . . . To hell with your movement. We're fed up with your movement. You're forcing us into it. We'll have to kill you."

An ad salesman in Chicago: "I'm getting to feel like I'd actually enjoy going out and shooting some of these people, I'm just so goddamned mad."

One, two, three, four, we don't want! your fucking war!

They gathered around the monument, on the wet grass, Dionysiac, beaded, flinging their clothes away. New England, Midwest, Southwest, cupfuls of innocents leave the city and buy farmland. At the end of the frontier, their backs to the briny Pacific, buses of tourists gape at the acid-dropping children in the San Francisco streets. A firebomb flares. An electric guitar bleeds.

Camus: "I would like to be able to love my country and still love justice."

Some years earlier, my two daughters were born, one in Wisconsin at a progressive university hospital where doctors and staff behaved affectionately, one in England where the midwife was a practical woman who held onto my feet and when she became impatient with me said: PUSH, Mother. Therefore I thought I knew what childbirth was supposed to be: a woman *gives birth* to a *child*, and the medical folk assist her.

But in the winter of 1970 I had arrived five months pregnant in Southern California, had difficulty finding an obstetrician who would take me, and so was now tasting normal American medical care. It tasted like money. During my initial visit to his ranch-style offices on a street where the palm trees lifted their heads into the smog like a row of fine mulatto ladies, Dr. Keensmile called me "Alicia" repeatedly, brightly, benignly, as if I were a child or a servant. I hated him right away. I hated his suntan. I knew he was untrue to his wife. I was sure he played golf. The routine delivery anesthetic for him and his group was a spinal block, he said. I explained that I would not need a spinal since I had got by before on a couple of cervical shots, assumed that deliveries were progressively easier, and wanted to decide about drugs myself when the time came. He smiled tolerantly at the ceiling. I remarked that I liked childbirth. I remarked that childbirth gave a woman an opportunity for supreme pleasure and heroism.

He smiled again. They teach them, in medical school, that pregnancy and birth are diseases. He twinkled. Besides, it was evident that he hated women. Perhaps that was why he became an obstetrician. Just be sure and watch your weight, Alicia. Smile.

I toyed, as I swelled and bulged like a watermelon, with the thought of driving out into the Mohave to have the baby. I continued my visits to Dr. Keensmile. I did not talk to Dr. Keensmile about Cambodia. I did not talk to him about Kent State. *Sauve qui peut.* You want a child of life, stay away from psychic poison. In the waiting room I found pamphlets which said that a newborn baby must be fed on a strict schedule, as it needed the discipline, and that one must not be moved by the fact that it would cry at first, as this was good for it, to start it out on the right foot. And my daughters were laughing at me for my difficulty in buckling their sandals.

In labor, I discovered that 1 could have an enjoyable time if I squatted on the bed, rocked a little while doing my breathing exercises, and sang songs in my head. The bed had muslin curtains drawn around it; nobody would be embarrassed by me. So I had settled into a melody and had been travelling downstream with it for some long duration, when a nurse came through the curtains, stork white, to ask if I was ready for my shot. Since the pains were becoming strong and I felt unsure about keeping control through the transitional stage of labor, which is the hardest, I said fine, expecting a local. This would temporarily alleviate the pain of the fast-stretching cervix, leaving other muscles free.

Of course, it was a sedative. I grew furry. They lay me down. I was eight fingers dilated, only five or seven minutes away from the final stage of labor, where a woman needs no drugs because she becomes a goddess. Then Dr. Keensmile appeared to ask if I was ready for my spinal. A faint flare of "no" passed, like a moonbeam. Because of the Demerol, if they had asked me whether I was ready to have my head severed, I probably would have said yes.

Drool ran from my mouth. Yes, I said.

When they wheeled me to the delivery room, I fought to maintain wakeful consciousness despite the Demerol, and fought to push, with my own body, to give birth to my child myself, despite the fact that I could feel nothing—nothing at all—below the waist, as if I did not exist there, as if I had been cut in half and bandaged.

A stainless place. I am conscious, only my joy is cut off. I feel the stainless will of everyone. Nothing red in the room. I am sweating. Death.

The black-haired head, followed by the supple limbs, emerges in the mirror. The doctor says it is a boy. Three thoughts fall, like file cards. One: Hooray! We made it! Finito! Two: YOU SONOFABITCHING BASTARD, NEXT TIME I'M GOING TO DO THIS RIGHT. Three: What next time?

Our bodies and our minds shoot into joy, like trees into leaves. Playfulness as children, sex, work with muscles, work with brains. Some bits survive, where we are lucky, or clever, or we fight. The world will amputate what it can, wanting us cripples. Cut off from joy, how many women conceive? Cut off, how many bear? And cut, how many give birth to their children? Now I am one of them. I did not fight. Beginning a day after my son's birth, and continuing for a week, I have swordlike headaches, which I attribute to the spinal. I am thirty-three. In the fall I will be back at work, back East. My husband and I have two daughters, both all right so far, and now the son for whom we were hoping. There will never be a next time.

What does this have to do with Cambodia?

VI.

SEX (EDUCATION)

baby, light my fire

Sally Lipton Derringer

After the Gold Rush

> *Don't let it bring you down,*
> *It's only castles burning,*
> *Just find someone who's turning,*
> *And you will come around*
> —Neil Young

Incense burning in the dorm room, my
        Exceptional Ed
books on the floor, my suitemates
        at the protest rally
voicing their beliefs about being in a
        country
where we did not belong, insisting on
        immediate withdrawal.
Neil Young on the stereo, *Guess Who's*
        Coming to Dinner
ending on TV, Katharine Hepburn
        standing up
to Spencer Tracy, their children making
        wedding plans.
I was saving myself for marriage like all
        my high school
friends, unlike the Down Syndrome
        women in my
textbooks, unlocking my door each night
        to a view
of my roommate Berty's naked feet at the
        end of the bed,
Linwood's or Germaine's or Tyrone's
        positioned

in-between. But that morning singing the
        words to
I Believe in You, all I could think was
        the smell

of patchouli, Lewis' workshirt on the
        chair,
the zipper of my fraying jeans mysteriously
        parting
and my legs agreeing, while I missed my
        9 o'clock
Philosophy of Self-Identity, the test on
        Plato's
Myth of the Cave, and castles burned
        magnificently
on the turntable, the oil from Lewis' Afro
        leaving
its mark on my white pillow, perfectly
        visible
in the light of the new study lamp my
        parents
had sent me up to school with, my education
        taking an
exceptional, unexpected turn.

Alberto Ríos

Like This It Is We Think To Dance

Hips to hips Elvis in our hearts the hearts
  Beating in our legs, Portuguese in our mouths
    We dance the slow dance of trees-near-fire frenzy
      The crawl of silk worm, the band beginning down a blouse
      The slow that wants to be fast
        That could be lovemaking

Hips to hips swaying we touch ourselves
  To ourselves in a toast of slow champagnes
    Our eyes swaying, with a view pendulums must have
      Swaying even with spring trees and light wind
        Swaying, forth and back, back then push
          Point to point and we do not break

Hips to hips hit of the champagne glass we put ourselves
  To ourselves forward, in that going way of terrier snout
    There after a mouse in the field, but slow
      An elephant, doing the last circus work of the night
        Head-strong still: *Saturnino el magnífico*
          Putting away, pushing against the backdrops and boxcars

Hips into the night away swaying still with the thinking
  Of the grocery store horse ride of our being five
    Of the nickel and the slot and the waiting and the bucking
      Jukebox of our bodies, Like this it is we think to dance
        Jump in our legs the legs our hard tongues are, running
          Into each other with the fingers of our ten hands on us

Susan Firer

Saint Valentine's Day, 1967

My mother said "What
would make you do it?" when
she heard I spent my fresh-
man year at college St. Valentine's
evening dancing at Waupun's
prison for the criminally insane.

What made me do it? I do
not know. I saw a sign-
up sheet on my way to sociology
class and I signed up.

I didn't know anyone else
on the yellow bus. It was snowing
when we entered the prison gates.
The prison looked like a castle:
turrets guards weapons, & walls.

There were rules first.
Often there are
rules first. We listened. I
listened carefully. In between
dances we were to stand
on opposite sides of the gymnasium.

We were not allowed to dance
twice with the same prisoner. We
were to dance a "decent"

distance from our partner. No one
was to give their last name
or address to anyone else.

This all sounded reasonable.
My epiphany from that night
long ago was: The
criminally insane are not reasonable!!!

The first thing they'd ask: "What's
your name? Where do you live?"
What would make them do it? I'd think
later, remembering the way they'd pull
my body into theirs, a way no
boy I'd known yet was aware of.

After each dance, most of my partners
would not let go, as if they didn't trust
there'd be another
dance. The guards would reappear:
"Go to your side of the gym." None
of my partners would. It was like musical
chairs: the process of elimination. Each
man they unwrapped from me disappeared.
The ones who stayed whispered awful

things into my ear, which they were
certainly not a "decent" distance from:
"Crowbar ... hair ... hole ... torn ...
solitary." Most of them talked sex
slang that I didn't know
had one thing to do with sex

because I was seventeen
& wearing a red-wool, A-line, Saint

Valentine's mini-dress. My dorm
would nominate me for snow carnival
princess the following week, but that night
I was dancing with the criminally insane,

where men smelled like nothing I recognized
and spoke a language I did not know.
The guard, who pried a particularly intense
prisoner from me (think *African Queen*:
Humphrey Bogart pulling leeches
off his body), asked: "How old are you?"

I said feeling away from home
full grown: "17!" He
looked me over, sucked his lips
and said: "Yeah well Miss Seventeen,
you just had yourself a slow dance with Ed Gein."*

* *Ed Gein was a notorious Wisconsin murderer and grave*
robber.

Tim Seibles

Delores Jepps

It seems insane now, but
she'd be standing soaked
in schoolday morning light,
her loose-leaf notebook,
flickering at the bus stop,
and we almost trembled

at the thought of her mouth
filled for a moment with both
of our short names. I don't know
what we saw when we saw
her face, but at fifteen there's
so much left to believe in,

that a girl with sunset
in her eyes, with a kind smile,
and a bright blue miniskirt softly
shading her bare thighs   really
could be *The Goddess*. Even
the gloss on her lips sighed
Kiss me   and you'll never

do homework again. Some Saturdays
my ace, Terry, would say, "Guess
who was buying Teaberry gum
in the drugstore on Stenton?"
And I could see the sweet
epiphany still stunning his eyes

and I knew that he knew
that I knew he knew   I knew—
especially once summer had come,
and the sun stayed up till we had
nothing else to do but wish
and wonder about *fine sistas*

in flimsy culottes and those *hotpants!*
James Brown screamed about: Crystal
Berry, Diane Ramsey, Kim Graves,
and *her*. This was around 1970: Vietnam
to the left of us, Black Muslims
to the right, big afros all over my

Philadelphia. We had no idea
where we were, how much history
had come before us—how much
cruelty, how much more dying
was on the way. For me and Terry,
it was a time when everything said

maybe, and maybe being blinded
by the beauty of a tenth grader
was proof that, for a little while,
we were safe from the teeth
that keep chewing up the world.
I'd like to commend

my parents   for keeping calm,
for not quitting their jobs or grabbing
guns   and for never letting up
about the amazing "so many doors
open to good students." I wish

I had kissed
Delores Jepps. I wish I could
have some small memory of her
warm and spicy mouth to wrap
these hungry words around. I

would like to have danced with her,
to have slow-cooked to a slow song
in her sleek, toffee arms: her body
balanced between the *Temptations'*
five voices and me—a boy annointed

with puberty, a kid with a B
average and cool best friend.
I don't think I've ever understood
how lonely I am, but I was

closer to it at fifteen because
I didn't know anything: my heart
so near the surface of my skin

I could have moved it with my hand.

Tim Seibles

Terry Moore

Our moms got us together at *Woolworth's,*
remember? Cheeseburgers. Summertime. 1967:
Twelve years in the world, mostly we burned

for football, to get it and move, to shake anybody
that wanted to bring us down: six points
was all we needed and time to find the future

where we'd be bad-ass superstars. We thought it was
hard, being young with adults running things, and it
got harder   not to think about girls and which words

would bring them close to our hands. Miniskirts:
remember *checkin' the cheese* in study hall—Marna
Evans—we had no idea where those legs could lead.

If it weren't for movies and the legends
of our big brothers we might never have believed
in smooth whispers, long kisses and maybe, even now,

we'd be dreaming only football—the rough touch
of leather tightly laced, grabbed and carried
to a place where men danced with nothing

to explain—the end zone, the promised land—and who
could blame us for craving such a simple destination?
Then came Joanie and for me it was Jane: short hugs,

slow songs, their mouths swimming into our mouths.
Among the Philly brothers, the word was "swag."
Did you swag on her, we'd ask, supposing the wet

dream of lips. *How many times did y'all swag:* so new,
the French kiss, the perfect neighborhood for anyone
as crazy and blue-balled as boys blazing on the verge

of the verge of their lives. Man,

we spent years on the phone daring each other
not to be young, not to be afraid of whatever
sex might mean. That paperback you found, *Nurse*

Nadine—the way she treated her patients: (what
exactly *was* a blow-job   and how long would it be
till we knew?) Our fathers were scary men—younger

than we are now—and ready to make themselves *clear*
without saying anything, especially when we got too cool
to listen, too big to hear. Did they believe in sex

the way we were starting to? Was there some secret living
softly inside their fists? My father loved my mother.
It looked so simple: year after year, the kiss

goodbye after breakfast, the kiss hello about five,
conversation at dinner, TV until time for bed.
It's pretty clear   I didn't know much

about my parents—just that they were usually
nice people and mostly on my side, and this
makes me wonder just how blind I'm gonna be,

'cause these days, I hardly see anything
the way I saw things back then   and, brah,
my eyes are wide open. The NFL will never

see us: I can't do half the moves we used to do—
loose-leg lean, that cutback stutter: short grass
lit beneath our simmering feet—but I'm glad

these forty years have found us still friends,
that we played some football and watched each other
break slowly into men   which is what we are by now,

which was always what we thought we really wanted.

Andrea Potos

To Want the Man

On Friday nights we were primed, my mother and I,
for *The Tom Jones Show* on TV.
We found our places—she in the wide blue
chair with a stool for her legs: me,
lying on the braided rug, my toes clutching
the wood-paneled edge of the TV.
The couch where my father sat
stayed empty again,
as if waiting for Tom Jones himself
to leap through the screen
and be ours.
In his black spray-on pants, his silk shirt,
his chest hairs spilling
over his thick gold chain, he'd sing:
It's not unusual to be loved by anyone,
It's not unnatural to have fun with anyone...
then he'd slide in his black boots
to the rim of the stage as if it were the rim of the world
where he appeared about to fall
into the waiting women's arms, but, always at the last second,
kept his own balance on stage
while they screamed and nearly fainted
to touch the hem of his pants,
to catch a sweat-drenched hanky
he might toss down.
My mother and I,
we were with these women all the way—

we knew the pitch of their longings,
we knew what it meant
to want the man
who belonged to every woman,
to no woman at all.

Kent Newkirk

Sex Education

Small town. Summer of Love. 1967.
In Boston, the Yaz-jazzed Red Sox
won the pennant, giving boys my age
reason to believe in Impossible Dreams,
even as the world seemed in such a rush
to explain the facts of life to a generation
of us intent, for once, on learning.

White-steepled church of plain-sense variety—
one aisle lined with junior high boys,
across the void, that cult from another world
called girls—we, the chosen few, sat united
as one in our desire for salvation from whatever sins
landed us in those pews and that uptight position.

Some Catholics, some Jews, and a few True Believers
mixed in, but most of us were Protestant white mutts,
all cursed by permission slips signed by parents over 30,
who even back then we knew better than to trust.

Pencils, paper, curiosities in hand, we listened by coercion
to Rev. What's-His-Face, the new guy with long hair—
what did we call them back then? Beatles, mop tops,
freaks? While our Christian fathers labeled them
hippies, pinkos, limp wrists, and stinking commies.

But Brother What's-His-Name kept his face straight
when he told us—as if from God's own mouth—
we would remain anonymous if we wrote down

and passed to him any questions we had about love,
about love between man and a woman,
about physical love, making love,
sexual intercourse. . .
sex. . .
and he, of course, would deliver us
the answers we were looking for.

So, of course, it took my buddies about two seconds
to give me a sideways glance of faith daring me
to take the bait. Foisted on his own cross,
that sex messiah was squirming
when I tossed him a question like an apple
with a worm in it. "If you get inside a woman,"
I posed, "is it possible to get stuck?"

Now, my love, my religion is you,
and I know, of course, the answer
he choked on is, of course.
"Of course!"

Martha Serpas

In Praise of the Passion Mark

First the unintentional: raspberry
blush, many-speckled lights,
and the message: *oops, sorry.*

Then the hard mark of the all-nighter,
a true Hoover, a hole black as leather
daring you to plummet.

We were dancing, it just happened,
she said, helplessly sentenced
to a week of turtlenecks

in May, in the sticky South. The frozen
spoon failing, she took a curling iron
to her neck and still her mother knew

the mix of teeth and lips and love.
Alone, she admired her shoulder's
violet smear: she was wanted

and had wanted. She'd have it
needled and inked, a permanent
badge of desire, a license for love.

And when the plaid-clad chem teacher
appeared with his bright bruise,
news traveled fast: wanting

does not die after all, after age,
one sort of taking in does not
supersede another. Go

for the jugular. We cannot
be sucked
dry.

Richard Wilbur

Playboy

High on his stockroom ladder like a dunce
The stock-boy sits, and studies like a sage
The subject matter of one glossy page,
As lost in curves as Archimedes once.

Sometimes, without a glance, he feeds himself.
The left hand, like a mother-bird in flight,
Brings him a sandwich for a sidelong bite,
And then returns it to a dusty shelf.

What so engrosses him? The wild décor
Of this pink-papered alcove into which
A naked girl has stumbled, with its rich
Welter of pelts and pillows on the floor,

Amidst which, kneeling in a supple pose,
She lifts a goblet in her farther hand,
As if about to toast a flower-stand
Above which hovers an exploding rose

Fired from a long-necked crystal vase that rests
Upon a tasseled and vermillion cloth
One taste of which would shrivel up a moth?
Or is he pondering her perfect breasts?

Nothing escapes him of her body's grace
Or of her floodlit skin, so sleek and warm
And yet so strangely like a uniform,
But what now grips his fancy is her face,

And how the cunning picture holds her still
At just that smiling instant when her soul,
Grown sweetly faint, and swept beyond control,
Consents to his inexorable will.

Paul Ruffin

Billy's Rubbers

Mornings at our swimming hole Billy Potts
would dump his find from a candy sack:
fresh rubbers from Lovers' Lane, most
with a great pearl of sperm in the head.
He washed them with the care of a mother,
dried them on blueberry limbs, and
folded them into their little boxes.

When one day we found his hoard in an
old abandoned barn, on a loft sill,
stack after stack of bright flat boxes
the size of match folders, each with
a girl's name lettered on the end,
we laughed and opened them, throwing
rubbers about like so much chaff,
flinging them among rafters and joists.
Ghost after little ghost drifted
and clung obscenely above our heads
or collapsed in the hay at our feet.
"What have you done, what have you done!"
he shrieked when he found us there, his
careful secret scattered about the loft.
In the soft light of that barn he picked
each one up, lovingly, naming them as he
folded them into their little boxes,
each Sarah and Jane and Susan.

We left him there, crouched
in the corner of the loft, his bright
boxes scattered about him like a child's
building blocks, his eyes wild
with the awful ghosts of love.

VII.

DRUGS AND
ROCK 'N' ROLL

dance beneath the diamond sky

Alan Shapiro

Mud Dancing

Woodstock 1969

Anonymous as steam in the steam teased
From the mud-hole at the field's edge
Where we were gathered, the unhallowed dead,

The herded up, the poured out like water,
Grew curious about us—naked as they were
Once, our numbers so like theirs,

And the air too, a familiar newsreel
Dusk of rain all afternoon.
It could almost have been themselves

They saw, except that we were dancing
Knee deep in mud, in the muddy
Gestures of their degradation,

Unpoliced and under no one's orders
But the wiry twang and thump
We danced to, sang to, yowling

On all fours, hooting on backs and bellies,
Smearing black lather over our own,
Each other's face, arms, hip

And crotch till we were sexless, placeless,
The whole damp mesh of who we were that made us
Strangers to each other, the shalts and shalt

Nots of you and me, mine and not yours,
Cast off easily as clothing
Into the blurred shapes of a single fluency.

Was this some new phase of their affliction?
The effect of yet some new device—
To make them go on dreaming, even now,

Some version of themselves so long accustomed
To their torment that they confused
Torment with exaltation, mud with light?

Frau History, they asked, *is this the final*
Reaving of what we loved well, that we should
Swarm now in the steam over the indistinguishable

Garments scattered everywhere in piles, that
We should need, even now, to sort through them,
To try to lift in our vaporous hands

The immovable rough granite
Of this sleeve or collar, that vest,
Those sandals, the flimsiest top?

Bryce Milligan

Song for a Highway Angel

for Nicki B.

She's a highway angel,
a danger to all who
travel down this road.
She's free falling
all in rags, living
Andy Warhol's code
for brilliant but studied
indifference.

She wants to watch
the world go by,
to shyly stare it down.
She wants the Haight
and Bleeker Street,
to be hip and poor downtown
in her brilliant but studied
indifference.

She wants to beg,
sing her songs for dimes,
wants to be a philosopher queen.
She wants to wage
her inner peace
against boredom's sheen
of brilliant but studied
indifference.

Implicit lies
and vacant eyes
are just a disguise she wears
but deep inside
it's hard to hide
how much it hurts to care.
So she wears
her mask
of indifference,
prays that her
brilliance
will make
a difference.

Lorna Dee Cervantes

Cream

> *I'm so glad. I'm so glad.*
> *I'm glad. I'm glad. I'm glad.*

Glad to be young in the vat,
proud in a hat, splayed out
on the mat of the future.
"I'm so glad. . ."—but far
away boys were dying, splat
on the fat face of farce
and the market of foreign
frenzy. It was all about rice
or flowers. Opium and the sweet
meat of free sex. *I'm so glad.*
I'm so glad. I'm glad. I'm glad.
I'm glad. But it was all about
balling in the ballroom. Love
and anarchy keeping the
wind from your hair—NOT.
It was glad not to be hungry
but fasting. Glad to be fast,
to not be left behind,
scribbled from history
in a quest for meat,
the beast before
the cream.

Vivian Shipley

Charlie's Asleep at the Wire
Waiting for You to Sleep

Your weekly poems were reruns: the prisoners of pirates walking
the plank. In San Francisco, you jumped, hiding long black dreds
under a red bandanna to imitate your father who tied one around

his head, dipped in blood from bodies that could not deny him.
At ten, lighting up Camels without filters, you knew hands didn't
leave the same marks as a belt. Dope sick at Thanksgiving, you

ranted about nine months of signing a yellow visitor pad printed
in black: National Center for Post Traumatic Stress Disorder.
Your hands in jeans to stop the shaking, a night watch belched

you down white tile threading a beige corridor. Your father sat
on paper sheets that ripped with weight, holding a Dixie cup
of orange juice for his pills. Once pythons, his arms were

stems, leafed in scars latticed over crosses, death unit insignias.
Fingering a necklace of withered ears beaded by kidney stones,
he would start with sweat on skin, then the helicopter droning

like the West Haven VA ventilation system, the elephant grass.
Predictable, your father ended with the tiger cage, boasting about
earning his blood bandanna again, again. A gallon of Dewars

every two days did not drown drums from your father's funeral
that you kept sounding out on a xylophone of bones he brought
to your mother from razor mountains in Pleiku, South Vietnam.

Bill, in April, sitting on rocks at Morgan Point, my words lifted
you. Caught in a down draft, you'd be drawn back, comparing
birds to chalk, undissolved by the wave's tongue, to the pill

you found too bitter to chew: your father stalking, spearing
shadows, leaving holes for eyes. Unerring as gulls plunging
onto the mussels they had dropped, going back to New Haven

in the back seat of my car, I knew you'd shoot up, probing
until you found a vein that would open, to feel that rush
you needed to keep Charlie at the wire, to keep you from sleep.

Aliki Barnstone

In the Workshop

That was the September when Berkeley was still novel
        and I took photos of my new Earth: the crowd of us
sprawled on the Plaza's brick because there on the Mario Savio Steps
        Allen Ginsberg wore a long golden tie, played his harmonium
on a plastic chair, and sang "Tyger, tyger burning bright."
        A few chosen poets stood around the sage's throne,
each taking his turn, and our friend from the workshop read
        the poem we already knew was too beautiful
and too lacerating, the tracks on their arms
        a map of shivers, the no-walls sex
they'd have anyplace, their glorious climb
        to Inspiration Point at dawn—
the sun orange enough to eat,
        uneaten oranges in their hands,
unoffered in the temple
        heroin made of their bodies.
Then their stroll downhill was more
        a free-fall or swan song over the Bay—
how mesmerizing the waters' surface
        where sun-glare whirled with fathomless
blues all the way to the Golden Gate
        and anywhere they'd find
to crash—a mat of redwood
        needles, some friends' itchy mattress
in the flatlands, cardboard laid on concrete
        below an underpass near the Marina.
When he read aloud, I wanted the high
        to be metaphor—painlessness is a form

of radiance, only words, not the body
  of the poet wasting away. And if underlying
his lines we detected disease, we were helpless to address it.
  If I wanted, I'd remember what I called him clearly
as his attentive expression and thin body leaning in close
  as I read my poem—my forgetfulness won't disturb his state—
and if he heard his name he might turn back
  to Earth from the high place where the dead go.

Dave Parsons

Austin Relativity

for Fred Hanna, Eddie Peterson, Bobby Jones, Donnie Parsons—
and all the Barton Springs Lifeguards of the Sixties

The old flagship Night Hawk Restaurant sits at a memory axis—
just over the Colorado River Bridge where Riverside Drive crosses

South Congress running east toward the Bergstrom Air Force Base;
where, at the guarded entrance, the large painted water tank spouted

PEACE IS OUR PROFESSION, the home of Dr. Strangelove's
bombers of the sixties; and later, those chillingly beautiful aquiline

Phantom jets streaking over the emerald hill country rolls
in the seventies and eighties; this same road ran west past the lazy

hills of Barton Springs, where those stunningly free living hippie
sprites would play and lay topless, sprawled across the lush

north green banks. . . across from the icy blue pumping methodical
flow of the springs that fronted my guard stand, appearing

at times as bodies strewn like casualties of some insidious sun
bomb, as I sweltered in baby oil mixed with the bold blood

of iodine, squinting over small patches of zinc oxide, musing
to the radio sounds of the Stones, Dylan, the many varied

voices that pumped with steely laced drum beats a music
into the heart of our turbulent days, instilling an urgent urge

to physically act—to escape from the stagnant pools of our youth,
to dive into the current of whitewater energy of the times, swim

that dark and intoxicatingly mystery, that dangerous rushing, rushing—

Alicia Ostriker

Satisfaction

Turn on the XM radio
listen to sixties rock
what better way to be
running out the clock

It brings me back to the dance floor
brings me back to the fire
with Stones and Jimi and Steppenwolf
we used to get higher and higher

they were napalming kids in Asia
we didn't know what for
thought if we loved each other
we'd put an end to war

guitar strings twisted electronic
we climbed like a rope or a breath
or a green beanstalk while Joy
took the mike with her partner Death

hot bodies out on the dance floor
doing what bodies do
in freedom and art and terror
stayin' alive, it's true

we thought minds could be altered
we thought the times were changed
the man was skinning the drum
the saxophone was deranged

yeah turn on the XM radio
listen to sixties rock
no better way to be
running out the clock

Kent Newkirk

Tripping Through Life, Fantastic!

One thing about tripping on '60s acid was, all circuits
were *Crosstown Traffic*. No matter how whacked out
you were in one world, you might be right on in the next.

Describing it is like trying to talk after a long day
packing more paycheck than poetry. Just because I mumble
through dinner, ignoring the price you've paid on your knees
precious as this handpicked salad doesn't mean I'm more focused
on dessert than I am on you. I'm of parallel minds, one graceful
and open–that's my mouth closed as I listen—the other trippin',
OD'n on small talk, stoned numb by polite conversation.

There are times I can't greet you properly in the parlor
of our shared heart because in my attic mind I'm in that
Purple Haze Hendrix played so clear. Just because
he sang it best doesn't mean a melting wall of generations
left behind aren't still wailing purple blues without him.

What I'm trying to say, what I'm trying to make vivid
as an acid trip featuring Frodo before he went Hollywood
and made it big as some movie star messiah, is that I love you,
I've always loved you, and long past the day we met and pledged
to meet again and again, I have lived to always love you.

But between us? As much we wish, we know flashbacks are myth,
and hobbits aren't the only ones chased by Gollums in the quest
to possess and cast off rings, so, it's trippy these days
conjuring an age it seems from this distance never existed,
like, if you remember the '60s, you weren't there.

The wrinkle in '60s acid is, unless you ate two hits, too,
you cannot imagine the trails loosed from these fingers.
The thing about love is, one hit of the lure of being there
and you're hooked on a high that constricts
even as it's ever-expanding.

Dave Parsons

Night Hawk

Congress Avenue rolls south from the Paramount Theater straight
through sentries of Live Oak over the Colorado River before it
        was a lake—

over that first main bridge before it housed the dark cloud of bats
and past the flagship Night Hawk Restaurant, where, I remember

running head to chest into President Lyndon Johnson as
his secret service agents, holding the glass doors open,

looked on in horror at the unexpected possibilities
of our collision, as I swung into the double doors

like some unexpected and inescapable event in Asia,
from the snaky nook of the restroom corridor, unaware

of his incoming entourage—s'cuse me—no, pardon me!
For a brief moment we did that uncertain dance to squeeze

by each other in the small vestibule of the double door entry, LBJ
in trapped composure, I imagine, with steak or a beer on his mind—

I—in awkward and puzzled wonderment—secret service agents
on the outside and inside doors—staying stiffly cool-sizzling—

Edward Hirsch

Days of 1968

She walked through Grant Park during the red days of summer.
One morning she woke up and smelled tear gas in her hair.

She liked Big Brother and the Holding Company, Bob Dylan,
Sly & the Family Stone, The Mothers of Invention.

When Jimi Hendrix played *Purple Haze* in a Jam Session
she had a vision of the Trail of Tears and the Cherokee Nation.

She dropped acid assiduously for more than a year.
She sang, "I want to take you higher and higher,"

and dreamt of cleansing the doors of perception.
After she joined the Sky Church I never saw her again. . .

Days of 1968, sometimes your shutters open
and I glimpse a star gleaming in the constellations.

I can almost reach up and snag her by the hand.
I can go to her if I don't look back at the ground.

Tim Hunt

Ravi Shankar After the Show

(Ithaca, NY, December 1968)

—for Michael Fremer who was there

In the back booth at HoJos, Ravi Shankar
Is eating fried clams and smoking an unfiltered
Cigarette as if he is inhaling its truth—
A traveling salesman pulled off the road. Another
Night, another show, another flight, as the empty
Children inhale the incense that floats the carpet
Off the stage—the mobius loop of tabla beats,
The sarong's keen a ground that is, too, horizon
And endless, and the sitar says now and the strings
Begin dancing his fingers—light dazzle off
Rippled water, jasmine, the night insects
As the moon rises. So many nows. That one,
This. The clams greasy and sweet
Answering a different hunger.

Lucille Lang Day

The Trip

I swallowed the Orange Phoenix and rose
from the ashes of my old self after breakfast
one Saturday morning. Brilliant, new,
I flew alone through labyrinthine clouds.

I soared through sunlight and taffeta pools.
No way would I return to Earth
to hold Gil's clammy hand. I had no hands,
just wings encrusted with jewels.

Trees were leafy tapestries, thickly woven
with light. The world was vibrant: bright
seeds collided in midair and bloomed
into roses, sailboats and blizzards of sand.

Music was everywhere, surging out of me
like waves from a radiant sea.
Gil kept trying to pull my face toward his,
but of course I had no use for those dull lips.

Katherine Solomon

A Momentarily Subdued Foofaraw

Paisley drapes sighed in '68. It's true.
And hummed in shades of grape and orange.
Rooms did breathe. Walls
inhaled. The sky dropped down
steel-drum symphonies
of rhythm to transform the random thump
of rain. Things we knew once—
before we forgot everything
but what we'd been told—
reappeared
somewhat disguised.

One psychedelic afternoon
I looked up to see myself
standing in a doorway
directly across from where I was sitting,
at the same moment in time,
but at the opposite end of the flow
and upheaval of an ocean-
coloured carpet in Charlie's room
above the head shop.

Did that mean I could be doubly sure I was real?
Or did it cut my chances in half?
Laughter, loud as tap-dancers,
clattered across the floor of my mind,
then crashed into a wall of panic,

until the apparition in the doorway spoke—
a smoky utterance of copper and olive that took its time
winding around the room and other people's heads
before it reached my ears.

By then I could see
how the woman atomizing
into the doorframe's beaded curtain,
and becoming one
hundred thousand glittering particles

was really my best friend,
Niki, and not another
me at all, because when I spoke
at times like that it always sounded evergreen
and violet. Winking

and curling her top lip
to hold a fake mustache in place, she
tossed her hair over her left shoulder—
by which I knew she meant to say
how her long strange trip
to the kitchen for a glass of water
had been pleasant and safe and filled
with happy adventures. That's why

I soon found myself
standing by the same sink
with no memory of turning on
the tap, mesmerized
by a singing poster on the wall.
Maybe you remember the one.
It said, *Better Living Through Chemistry*
below a village-sized gathering

of smiling hippies on a sidewalk
in San Francisco. From the front row

a girl we used to know in Boston raised her voice
above the din and chorus of the song
that poured into the room.
She sang a mellow yellow solo
in couplets graceful as the matched fins
of flying fish. A song lovely
and menacing as any storm at sea.
I never knew Priscilla
could sing like that.

Now sometimes when I think I'm drowning
in perceptions, I remember
how I used to love to pile them on. And how
once I felt my body
was an island in an archipelago.
How once each breath
sounded like a soft hurrah
above the momentarily subdued foofaraw
of every day. And how for days on end
I could enter into being

everyone
or no one at all, just a twinkle
in the stream that ran through
strawberry fields forever
back in 1968.

Barbara Hamby

Ode to Rock 'n' Roll

Tonight the band is so good you have to dance, the lead
        singer's voice like honey at the bottom of a jar,
so deep your hand gets stuck, fingers skimming the last
        bead of sweet, so sticky you remember riding
in a car, an MG or midnight blue Mustang,
        through a fragrant tropical night, 1969 it was,
the radio playing "Ain't Too Proud to Beg,"
        only you were, didn't even know what begging was,
but now you know. Oh, you've done some begging
        in your time, been way down, so low you thought
you'd never get up, because you'd been that bad; you'd lied,
        cheated, stolen, or that's what the falsetto
is singing, swooping down like a crazy mockingbird
        after an alley cat, scratching your skin,
making your tired bones loose in their sockets, and you're
        shaking it, moving your hips like you was some kind
of home girl, jumping up like that skinny cat on a hot
        sidewalk. You're frying eggs, Mama, the bald drummer
telling you how to cut that particular rug into a thousand pieces,
        your feet religious, your knees like holy water,
head crazy with hair, the wild Indian your mother
        always said you were, but a Comanche, whose word
for themselves means *the human beings* and that's what you are,
        finally, in this sweltering room in the middle
of December, your arms moving like a semaphore,
        as if you were frantically trying to signal
a distant ship in the doom of the night, an ark filled
        with such fear the Bantu word *mbuki-mvuki,*

to tear off your clothes to dance, is almost lost till it floats
        back on the Mississippi as *boogie-woogie*
in a wild trance of forgetting, and sometimes the spot
        on your sullen heart is the sweetest part,
this collision of Bantu, blues, hillbilly riffs, riding the night
        like a wild stallion filled with a murderous longing.
Oh, let there be fire, a sulfurous kindling of earth and air,
        and in the clear morning may we all be Comanches,
riding the high plains of indifferent grass, fierce with the murmur
        of gods—Leadbelly's growl, Hendrix's response,
Little Richard's screams, heaven sent as our own voices
        were we human enough to heed the call.

Vivian Shipley

Hike Up Av. Du Pere-Lachaise

Smashed into francs, pounded into dirt, beer bottle
        caps carpet the space framing Jim Morrison's
grave. Yes, it's Paris, but it's not Dom Perignon,
        it's a keg party, another chance to chant *Toga,*
Toga, echo the Doors' *C'mon Baby Light My Fire*

that lures me. That, and the right to brag I fit
        into my old jeans embroidered with daisies
around the crotch, razored to look ripped out
        at the knees. Riding a Harley with James Dean,
I would never have squealed or begged to slow

down. Goading him to fly close to trees, guard rails,
        my feet tucked well away from burns and exhaust,
I'd ask my *Rebel Without a Cause* to shimmy back
        and fill space between my thighs so I could
forget where my body ended and his began. Barreling

out, *Freedom's just another word for nothing left to lose,*
        I still can do Janis Joplin, hang out, play acoustic.
No sod covers Jim Morrison's coffin, just soil mixed
        with fine gravel, a plastic red rose, a note from Stan.
Rectangular and flat, the stone is not original, is replaced

at least once a month whenever it's covered in graffiti:
        We love you, Jim from Edwin and Emile.
Beneath peace signs cut in the *O's* in *JAMES DOUGLAS,*
        1940-1971, it is enough for me that there is space
to carve my name where it will last, for a while.

Michael Waters

Christ at the Apollo, 1962

for Andrew Hudgins

Even in religious fervor there is a touch of animal heat.
—Walt Whitman

Despite the grisly wounds portrayed in prints,
the ropy prongs of blood stapling His eyes
or holes like burnt half-dollars in His feet,
the purple gash a coked teenybopper's
lipsticked mouth in His side, Christ's suffering
seemed less divine than the doubling-over
pain possessing "the hardest working man."
I still don't know whose wounds were worse: Christ's brow
thumb-tacked with thorns, humped crowns of feet spike-split—
or James Brown's shattered knees. It's blasphemy
to equate such ravers in their lonesome
afflictions, but when James collapsed on stage
and whispered *please please please,* I rocked with cold,
forsaken Jesus in Gethsemane
and, for the first time, grasped His agony.
Both rose, Christ in His unbleached muslin gown
to assume His rightful, heavenly throne,
James wrapped in his cape, pussy-pink satin,
to ecstatic whoops of fans in Harlem.
When resurrection tugs, I'd rather let
The Famous Flames clasp my hand to guide me
than proud Mary or angelic orders
still befuddled by unbridled passion.

Pale sisters foistered relics upon me,
charred splinter from that chatty thief's cross and
snipped thread from the shroud that xeroxed Christ's corpse,
so I can't help but fashion the future—
soul-struck pilgrims prostrate at the altar
that preserves our Godfather's three-inch heels
or, under glass, like St. Catherine's skull, *please,*
his wicked, marcelled conk, his tortured knees.

Jim Elledge

Strangers: An Essay

> Comment: "'Tom Cruise should not play Jim."
> Response: "He won't."
> —Graffiti, Pére Lachaise

Forget maps at 10F each. Those before
you left markers no birds carry off:
hundreds of Jims with arrows in hot
pink fingernail polish on crypt
sides or street signs from any cemetery
entrance or intersection to his grave
—6th Division, east of Abélard and
Héloïse's, east of the Crematorium.

I got lost in the boulevard-and-avenue
lattice then found by a Frenchman
who crossed my path, glanced
back, mumbled, "Morrison?", crooked his
finger at my *Mais oui,* and led me.

Three Dutch kids already there stood
silent as the slabs neighboring his, where
those before us scribbled,
 "Break on through to the other side,"
 "Come on, baby, light my fire,"
 "People are strange,"
to whom others answered,
 "Too drunk to fuck on this side,"
 "Jim, we want your babies,"
 "Let Jim live. Stay strange."

–graffiti as much props in acts of
devotion or contrition as Chartres'
stained glass or its stone floor maze
across which penitents crawl on their
knees, crossing themselves.

       Clairvoyants, the kids connect, however
they may, with the other side, scribbling
syllables meaning more to them and him
now than in two centuries, a dead
syntax musicologists or pop-culture freaks
will carbon date, translate, add as footnote
to treatises on an obscure Eastern
section of Paris or a shadowy American
prone to black leather and flashing
crowds, only more words gathering dust on
library shelves in world capitals.

       The man who found me sweeps the grave
daily, collects cigarette butts and pint
whiskey bottles left by those who
leave something of themselves
behind, what nourishes and harms
simultaneously, what Morrison would've
recognized, understood, maybe even
blessed had he risen as our breath rose,
white and formless that chilly morning.

       Then two more arrived, boys, Parisian,
one raven hair and raven eyes who sat
beside me, who–when a stray Calico
climbed into my lap, planted muddy paw
prints on my thighs, and jabbed his head
into my jacket arm pit–asked, "Know
his name?" then said, "Jim" when I shook

my head. He smiled at me, the stranger
here, the only one old enough to've watched
Morrison bare it for crowds, our peek
worth the ticket's cost, enough to keep
us horny and giggling for weeks.

   The boy began, "Come on, baby,
light. . ." One by one the rest added
their voices, pronunciation perfect, cadence
misplaced, a tinny choir. Before he could motion
me to join in, I rose into wisps of
my breath, divined north by where the sun
perched in trees, and left to leave
stones for Edith Piaf and Paul Éluard.
No graffiti or hymns for them
—only flowers, plastic or wilting.

Adrian C. Louis

Listening to the Doors

Listening to The Doors, radio blasting
& toking mind-bending hash & speeding
from Berkeley toward The City in Maya's
parents' paneled Ford wagon, he tripped
on the colony of driftwood sculptures
in the mud flats before the Bay Bridge.
The hash, the car, Jim Morrison & the eerie
sculptures pushed him toward panic.
Naatsi prayed for calm & reached
out to the small town of his desert mind.
He remembered always watching the pimpled
white kids leave his high school at three
& spin their parents' cars out of the parking
lot as disturbed as a nest of angry bees
searching for an invisible honey thief.

The Indian kids, too poor to own cars,
placed their feet upon the earth
& moped toward their future
or was it their past? They weren't
dreaming of Wovoka or Crazy Horse.
They were dreaming of a good used car
like Maya's parents' paneled Ford wagon.

Jim Daniels

Jimi Hendrix, National Anthem

Everybody read all this historic shit into it
when it was just Jimi stoned and messing
around. How many times have you listened
to it the whole way through? Everyone I knew
lifted the lone arm after the first few notes
like yeah, yeah, we get it Jimi. The song sucks
no matter what you do and this crazy notion
I feel at every sporting event is that if I don't take
my hat off somebody's gonna kick my ass so
I take it off and so does everybody else
many of whom probably were not wearing hats
back at Woodstock and had more hair then
but it's like we gotta do this now because otherwise
people will think we don't love our country
and all the soldiers who die for it though
nobody's whistling it as they work
if you know what I mean, right Jimi?
I'd take my hat off for "Wild Thing."

Edward Hirsch

The Burning of the Midnight Lamp

Listening to *Purple Haze* and *The Wind Cries Mary,*
Let Me Stand Next to Your Fire and *Manic Depression,*

I am drifting undersea toward strobe lights
and feedback, the dreamy, acoustic waves of 1969.

Remember how you explained those dirty sounds—
the two-note riff banned by the Spanish Inquisition,

the hammer-ons and pull-offs, the sharpened ninth?
Is it tomorrow or just the end of time?

I've forgotten nothing. Any moment I'll cross
the campus near the dormitory where you've moved in

with another man; I'll pause under the window trembling
with volume—a betrayer betrayed and turning back

to the raw, metallic, bristling taste of wind.
The morning is dead and the day is too

There's nothing left here to lead me, but the velvet moon
(you always liked the wah-wah pedal on that song).

. . .

Someone is playing *Voodoo Child* and *House Burning Down,*
checking the chord progression in *Spanish Castle Magic*

and the octaves in *Third Stone from the Sun*.
Another is blasting *Crosstown Traffic* from a lounge

where darkness branches into maroon rivers
and cigarette butts flare into the stars.

No more parties with our friends eating seeds
and lacing punch, smoking joints in a dim room

where you go on talking about sinister bent strings
and dive-bombing sounds, the devil invoked

in the interval of a tritone or flattened fifth.
No more waiting for you to return to me

(that forgotten earring lying on the floor)
through a downpour of left-handed notes.

But sometimes when I close my eyes
I see your body fading back into shadows.

. . .

As a child, Jimi Hendrix watched his soul floating
away from his torso, looking down at himself

from a different realm. He was awake but slipping
mindlessly through another dimension, the astral plane.

That's how you felt about LSD and STP,
those ten-milligram doses of the sublime.

We were looking for fire-escapes: ladders
and watchtowers spiraling up from the ground.

But that year as I smoldered within my body
and you tripped through the acid nights

Orpheus stomped microphones and humped speakers,
smashing amplifiers on stage after stage

as though he could whammy the Underworld
into submission and subdue the Furies

while darkness vibrated around him
and electric guitars exploded into flames.

VIII.

AFTERMATH

the answer, blowing in the wind

Hunt Hawkins

The Revolution in Oakland

Lucy filled the closet with pamphlets.
Jum and Winston refused to be housebroken.
Every night Lucy toked up on the penis pipe.
Our days were smoke.
Using piss from a pregnant friend,
Rory got on welfare.
Aggie slept in the backyard.
She found beauty in the decrepit house.
She wanted to feel right.
Something was stirring in the rented houses of the Bay Area.
The People's Peace Treaty. Produce Conspiracy.
Alex told us about the thirties.
His wife was dead. He cried.
The Brigade returned from Cuba,
smoking cigars.
I tried to write.
I wanted women to manage my feelings.
Aggie said I wasn't bad.
It's all right to cry.
We were trying to change ourselves.
Drinking Regal Beer,
we planned a garden, never planted.
Auto mechanics. First Aid.
We talked about Diana Oughton,
blown apart by her own bomb in New York.
The papers said her problems were personal.
Lucy said society was bad.

We learned karate.
Aggie said we were damaged inside.
We couldn't feel right.
Rory was caught shoplifting.
The stores were our enemy.
Packaging was bad.
Aggie cut off all her hair.
An apartment complex fills the lot
where our house once stood.
In 1970 we came apart.

Ted Kooser

Shame

You were a college student, a waitress
paying your way through the sixties,
and I was recently divorced, alone
and lonely, looking for someone to love
in those dreary years when it seemed
no one else was willing "to make
a commitment," as we said back then,
and I mustered my courage and asked you
to dinner, and met you at your door,
and we walked downtown, both of us shy,
both awkward, both scented and scrubbed
and overdressed and clopping along
in new and uncomfortable shoes,
and over wine and dinner, as we began
to feel more comfortable together,
sometimes touching each other's hands,
I told you my story and you told me yours,
the way young people will,
you finishing yours with the news
that you had leukemia, the slow kind
that with "adequate treatment"
could keep you alive, at least for a time,
and it frightened me, having no courage
for anyone's pain but my own, knowing
nothing at all about love, and surely
you must have been terribly hurt
to read all that in my expression,

and forty years later I'm still ashamed
to have been the kind of person
who could then walk you back to your door
still early in the evening, and leave you
there with a dry little kiss and a promise,
who would never phone, who would avoid
the restaurant where I'd first seen you
wiping the tables, working your way
through so much more than college,
you in your starched uniform apron
with a plastic tag pinned to your breast
and your name that I've even forgotten.

Vivian Shipley

Obeying Glands

We were rabbits before arthritis settled in our knees.
Not yet thirty, Summer of '67, Summer of Love,

The Doors' *Light My Fire* ran through our legs,
loosening them like dirt. The Beatles were total,

psychedelic, *Sgt. Pepper's Lonely Hearts Club Band.*
Ed, you and I had plans to live beyond all jurisdiction, be

right on with Jerry Garcia and The Grateful Dead, move
to Haight-Ashbury with Phil, Vince, Mickey, Bob, BK.

The point was never to be trapped by circumstance:
flaking paint the size of saltines, our dog retrieving

potatoes off the neighbor's grill, troweling out crabgrass.
I had been trained by the Appalachians not to step

into a hollow that could surprise the foot, and at sixty-one,
I still have my pride, won't hold the rail, plant both feet

on a step for balance. What memory has given to you
has not been taken, year by year, like an eraser working

bottom to top of the board: your VW van, *Broken Arrow,*
Candyman, Space. You still can rock just like you did,

a Deadhead, at the Renaissance Fair Grounds in 1972. Still,
for no apparent reason, our feet ache, neck and shoulders

never quite relax; this is not what we had in mind. Age
spots our hands like driftwood from Long Island Sound,

but buoying us up are Janis Joplin and Jimi Hendrix
rocketing The Monterey Pop Festival. Leather tooled

guitar strap, his chest bared, jacket open to his waist,
Jimi wore double chain link strands of what could have been

real gold. His medallion, the size of my fist, was a shield
emblazoned with the British lion. No talent, I dressed

like Jimi, had a jacket made with beaver lapels and cuffs,
braiding and beads on the front. Gilded cord on sleeves

writhing above four military stripes, I looked more like
John Philip Sousa. No chest hair, no Jimi Hendrix, I never

unhooked the front all the way down to my navel, just
enough to prod my mother into a *girls-like-me* rage. Janis,

Jimi, Jerry escaped. Not us. Staying alive, you still redline
our yellow Porsche, praying *Lord, won't you buy me*

a Mercedes Benz. Your hair gone, mine a red barn stenciled
in gray artifacts of euonymus, we keep on truckin' with

muscle that survived, thankful for fieldstones heaved by frost,
monuments to record our apple orchard that's gone to wood.

Judith Arcana

The Sun in Montana

Long ago in another life, a life before the one I'm living
now, I learned the hard way, the way of walking miles
to school, home again when it was late, already dark
shadows purple on the deep snow. That way. I learned
security is only in your head. It has no existence, no
meaning outside of you. Is that the only way to learn?
The hard way? Maybe that's how everybody learns
their lessons, simple as day: the sky is blue, the trees
green, the sun yellow, there's no such thing as security.
It's an idea, something to think, not something to have.
That life happened before we said *context* or *conditions*—
before *the thing itself* became impossible, before Heisenberg
got more popular than the Beatles: we could pretend.
We could ignore that absence, the absolute lack of security
in what is still called innocently ignorant blithely
unthinkingly: *the real* world—the place where
when I was seventeen, the president lied: a pilot (a man
too old to walk to school with me) shot down for lying
for spying; our country shot down by Russia for cheating
for sneaking, and the president lied. He said national security.
One short season that show played all the theaters. The lesson
had to come around again, repeat, review, repeat, remember
like a part in a play, like shooting an American
movie: black and white and color; back and forth in time
reviewing lessons of plot, character, crisis, climax.
In my other life we learned our parts, we said our lines
we acted the husband, the lover, the wife, played out
domestic miniatures of the nation: lying and being discovered.

We acted as if we could know, as if security was something
we could get, like orange juice out of the fridge
like a writ of habeas corpus, like a job when they were plenty
like glittering pebbles scattered across the wooden sill of a mine.

Ginny Lowe Connors

Reunion

and didn't Talia's brother get killed
        and didn't Cathy's brother bolt to Canada
though he wanted to stay in Hawaii, where he got married
        and didn't Patrick come home unable to look anyone
in the eye though he had been such a sweet funny boy
        and didn't Huxley, the high school jock, come back
only partially, the whites of his eyes yellow, his skin orange,
        his hands shaky and hasn't he always
had problems since but weren't most of us spared
        and weren't the chemical companies getting freaking rich
and didn't we march and march, carrying signs
        and didn't we chant while our cousins and brothers
were trained to kill and didn't we believe the suits would have to
        listen, they'd have to, if we were loud enough, if we
were strong enough if if if—and weren't we drunk with indignation
        and didn't we hitchhike to D.C.
more than once and weren't my shoes stolen as I slept
        beneath the Washington Monument, that colossal
finger raised to the world, and weren't there thousands
        of us glorious in our hair and our righteousness and didn't we
march carrying signs and didn't we chant, didn't we hear
        them screaming, see them running and catch sharp whiffs
of tear gas in the air but didn't that news photo of a little girl screaming
        and running naked toward us, everything burning
behind her, napalm, napalm, didn't that photo dissolve, didn't
        that child run right out of the papers and into our bones
and didn't we know we were the lucky ones and weren't we furious
        to have to carry that guilt and weren't we euphoric

with our refusals and weren't we terrified of our helplessness
        and weren't we smug and self-satisfied and filled with secret
doubts and weren't there a lot of cops on huge brown horses
        and didn't Daryl always call them fascist pigs but didn't
Megan refuse to do that 'cause her daddy was a cop and didn't
        the *Manchester Union Leader* call us all pinko commie punks
and didn't that delight us and didn't the reefers make the rounds
        and those sharp inhalations, the heat and the jangle that ached
as we strained to hold it, while passing it on, wasn't that like love
        but didn't somebody's brother drop something stronger
and fly off the roof and didn't we see a strange boy,
        stoned, staring up at the sun and weren't his eyes
turning into embers and didn't he shine his smile
        briefly upon us and didn't he look like a wild fallen angel
and didn't you bet he'd never make it to adulthood and didn't
        we feel a black disbelieving terror at the thought of ever becoming
middle-aged and baby, isn't that exactly where we've arrived

Leon Stokesbury

Evening's End: 1943-1970

For the first time in what must be
the better part of two years now
I happened to hear Janis
in her glory—
all that tinctured syrup
dripping off
a razorblade—
on the radio today singing "Summertime."

And it took me back to this girl I knew,
a woman really, my first year
writing undergraduate poetry
at the Mirabeau B. Lamar
State College of Technology
in Beaumont, Texas,
back in 1966.

This woman was the latest in a line,
the latest steady
of my friend John Coyle that spring—
and I remember she was plain:
she was short: and plain
and wore her brown hair up
in a sort of bun in back
that made her plainer still.

I don't know where John met her,
but word went round

she had moved back in with Mom and Dad
down in Port Arthur
to get her head straight,
to attend Lamar,
to study History,
after several years in San Francisco
where she had drifted
into a "bad scene"
taking heroin.

I was twenty,
still lived with Mom and Dad myself,
and so knew nothing
about "bad scenes,"
but I do remember once or twice
each month that spring
John would give a party
with this woman always there.
And always as the evening's end came on
this woman, silent for hours,
would reveal, from thin air,
her guitar,
settle in a chair,
release her long hair
from the bun it was in,
and begin.

Her hair flowed over her shoulders,
and the ends of the strands of hair
like tarnished brass in lamplight
would brush and drag across
the sides of the guitar
as this woman bent
over it.

How low and guttural, how
slow and torchlit, how
amber her song, how absolutely
unlike the tiny nondescript
a few minutes before—

And I remember also,
from later on that spring,
from May of that year,
two nights in particular.

The first night was a party
this woman gave
at her parents' home.
Her parents' home
was beige:
the bricks the parents' home
was built with
were beige.

The entire house was carpeted
in beige.
John's girl greeted everyone at the door,
a martini in one hand

and a lit cigarette
in an Oriental
ivory cigarette holder in the other,
laughing
for once, and tossing back
her long brown hair.

All the women wore
black full-length party dresses—
and I remember the young woman's father,

how odd he seemed
in his charcoal suit and tie,
his gray hair—
how unamused.

Then John Coyle was drunk.
He spilled his beer
across the beige frontroom carpet:
that darker dampness sinking in,
the father vanished
from the scene.

The next week we double-dated.
I convinced John and his girl
to see a double feature,
Irma La Douce and *Tom Jones,*
at the Pines Theatre.

And I can recall John's girl
saying just one thing that night.

After the films, John was quizzical,
contentious, full of ridicule
for movies I had guaranteed he would enjoy.
He turned and asked her
what she thought—
and in the softest
of tones, a vague rumor
of honeysuckle in the air,
she almost whispered,
"I thought they were beautiful."
That was the last time that I saw her,
the last thing that I heard her say.

A few weeks later,
she drove over to John's house
in the middle of the afternoon,
and caught him in bed
with Suzanne Morain,
a graduate assistant
from the English Department at Lamar.

John told me later
that when she saw them in the bedroom
she ran into the kitchen,
picked up a broom,
and began to sweep the floor—
weeping.

When John sauntered in
she threw the broom at him,
ran out the door,
got in her car and drove away.
And from that day on,
no one ever saw that woman
in Beaumont again.

The next day she moved to Austin.
And later on, I heard,
back to San Francisco.
And I remember when John told me this,
with a semi-shocked expression
on his face, he turned
and looked up, and said, "You know,
I guess she must have really *loved* me."

I was twenty years old.
What did I know?
What could I say?

I could not think
of anything to say,
except, "Yes,
I guess so."

It was summertime.

Thus runs the world away.

Kathleen Winter

Nostalgia for Apollo

Back then, back there, the handsome astronauts
could build their own machines,
each man assigned a wing, a plan, a system to design.
In their white shirts, in their thin ties, they worked it out.
At cocktail parties, on cocktail napkins
at the bar, they synchronized the rendezvous
of master ship with its squad module, or, alone
in their well-ordered minds, they engineered
the right thing for a man to say when stepping off
the last rung onto lunar dust, just after taking
a piss on the ladder. I miss their gravity-free
cantering across the fields of the moon,
their silent, patient waving from behind curved
glass, their close-cropped hair, their Mission Control cigars,
their guts. I miss their elevated heart-rates
at the takeoff, god-like, their views of Earth's
swirled atmosphere, their cowboy tendency
to terseness, their ticker-tape parades, their quaint
faith in our nation, their quaint male
universe in which I was a lovely
and a silent child.

Kate Daniels

Homage to Calvin Spotswood

> *Yet not for those,*
> *Nor what the potent victor in his rage*
> *Can else inflict, do I repent or change,*
> *Though changed in outward luster. . .*
> —Paradise Lost, Bk. 1

Because I couldn't bear to go back to the southside
of Richmond and the life I had led there–the blaring
televisions, the chained up hounds, the cigarettes hissing
in ceramic saucers, the *not never's, I'm fixin' to'gs,*
the *ain'ts*–because anything at all was better than that,
I took the job. The four bucks an hour, the zip-front,
teal-colored, polyester uniform, the hairnets and latex gloves,
the intimate odors of piss and sweat, the eight hour
nighttime shifts of vomitus and shit, of death and death,
and then more death. Each day I pinned on the badge that
         assigned me
to hell: nurse's aide on an oncology ward for terminal patients.

Calvin Spotswood was my first patient. His metal chart
proclaimed him: "Non-ambulatory, terminal C. A." A Goner,
the docs called him, a non-compliant asshole they wheeled
like a dying plant, out of the sun, out of the way
so he could wither and perish at his own speed distant from those
with happier prognosis.
They parked him in a dim back room so he could go unheard
when pain peeled him down to his disappearing center.

Calvin dropped down through a chute in the day to day,
and skidded in for a landing on the flaming shores
of Stage III colo-rectal cancer. Nightly, he cooked there,
flipping back and forth on the grainy, cloroxed sheets
like a grilling fish. Timidly at first, I bathed the hot grate
of his ribs with tepid water, the cloth I dipped
almost sizzling dry on his heaving chest. I hated the feel
of his skin, the intimacy of my hands on his body. I hated
to touch him—a dying man, a devil, trapped, alive, in hell.

I feel
uncomfortable now, because he was black, imagining
Calvin as Milton's Satan, as if I am demonizing him unfairly,
or engaging in a stereotype based on race. But I had read the poem
and recognized immediately the one who was "hurled headlong
        flaming"
from the gates of heaven, and "chained" for infinity "on the burning
        lake"
of his hospital bed. Like Lucifer, Calvin
was a troubling complex anti-hero—a horrible person in many ways,
        stubborn
and stupid, had abused his nurses and cursed the doctors,
refusing the colostomy that might have prolonged—or saved—his life.
He wouldn't be *unmanned*, he said, *shitting in a bag. No f-ing way.*
He said "f-ing," instead of the full blown word,
a kind of delicacy I found peculiar, and then endearing.
And though the tumor, inexorably, day by day, shut him down,
he wouldn't pray, or console himself in any of the usual ways. Each
        afternoon,
he turned away from the Pentacostal preacher who stood with
        his Bible
at the foot of his bed, and said his name kindly and asked to say
a prayer or lay his hands upon the burning body. *No f-ing way.*

The tumor grew until it bound itself into his stomach wall.
Each move he made extracted a fiery arrow of flaming pain
from his rotten gut. And when the house staff figured
they had him beat, and organized a betting pool on how soon
     old Calvin
would entrust himself to the surgeon's knife so he could eat
again, he still declined, still whined for pussy, porno mags,
and chicken fried in bacon grease. A third year resident,
Harvard M. D., wrote an order for the supper Calvin thought
he craved: mashed potatoes and buttered bread, a chicken-battered,
deep-fried steak. Beaming, our man consumed it while his doctor
     lingered
outside his door to await the inevitable result of natural process
of human digestion. . . . Here is where I need to remind you that this
was back when the old U. Va. hospital still stood, on the brick-
     curbed rim
of Hospital Drive, where the sign saying *Private* really meant white,
     a reminder
a reminder of what passed for health care in the segregated South.
Nurses still wore bobby-pinned, absurd white hats that looked
as if they were about to levitate off their heads.
The R. N.'s were white, the practicals, black.
And none of the docs, of course, were black.
But Calvin was, and the Civil Rights Act was a decade old,
so it was the New South, instead of the Old, where Calvin consumed

his last good meal, deluded into thinking that a black man in the
     South
had finally won. An hour later, he knew he'd lost, and patients
two floors down could hear him screaming from the mouth
of the flaming crater he filled with curses.

Night after night, wrist deep in the tepid water I bathed him with,
I stood at his bedside and tried to change him from hot to cool
and listened to him discourse manically on the mysteries of gender:

Born again, he'd be a woman in slick red panties, a streetwalking
whore in high-heeled sandals and torn, black hose, opening his legs
for paper money, filling his purse with bucks to spend.
How anyone was granted a life like that he could never comprehend:
getting paid to fuck. His greatest treasure had been a dark red
          Pontiac with bucket seats
he'd drive to D. C.'s 14ᵗʰ Street to look for whores and a game of cards.
He'd been a lumberjack, he revealed one night. A quelling job,
and measured with his hands sphered into a circle, the muscles
jettisoned to illness. His strength had been his pride.
Now, he was weary and diminutive, sick stick of a man,
shriveled by a tumor. The image of his former power resided
in the two huge wives who guarded his door, one white, one black.
Passing between the corporal portals of their womanly flesh,
my pale-toned puniness frightened me. But even in the final stages
of a violently invasive terminal carcinoma, nothing daunted Calvin–
not even the quarter ton of dominating, loud-mouthed women
with whom he had conceived six children. I marveled
at the unrancorous way they held each other, their cheap clothing
crinkling noisily, releasing that funky odor big people carry.
Their decalled fingernails, their huge, flopping breasts, their ornate
          hairdos–
the one teased up and lacquered high in place, the other cornrowed
flat with beads–their flamboyance so obvious I couldn't help
but apprehend what Calvin Spotswood thought was hot in women.
Not me, of course, skinny college girl with straight brown hair,
and wire-rimmed glasses, dog-earing Book I of *Paradise Lost*. . . .
What Calvin adored were the superfluous extras I tried to delete–
fat and loudness, clandestine odors of secreted musk.

At the end, cupping his withered, hairless testicles
in my cool, white palm because he asked me to, it wasn't anything
like witnessing a death. More like the birth of a new world, really,
he was entering alone. The little universe of sperm that twirled
beneath my hand, he was taking with him. On the burning bed,

his mouth lolled open in forgotten, wasted pleasure,
and I saw in my mind images of the South's strange fruit, the old photos
bound into books of black men who'd transgressed early in the century,
swinging heavily from trees–their demeaned postures and living deaths.
But Calvin was uncatalogued there. His name was written
in the *dramatis personae* of a slimmer text, an epic poem about the fall
from grace of a defiant, finger-flipping Beelzebub who dared
to challenge the creator of the world where black men swung
from the limbs of trees for admiring the backside of fair-skinned girls.

Calvin was the one kicking holes in the floor of that so-called
       heaven to hasten
his eviction. And so I touched him. I did, and stroked him even closer
to the edge, marveling at the force of a ravaged life, at the inscrutable
nature of a God who would keep alive a man who claimed to
       hate his f-ing guts
and nail into my mind forever, Calvin Spotswood in his final hours,
undiminished, unredeemed, unrepentant, his poor black body
       burning and burning.

Paul Mariani

The Things They Taught Me

i

Except on green rosters long since
gone to yellow, or asleep somewhere
in the vaults of Whitmore, most
of their names are lost to me,
covered palimpsest-wise by others
coming after, each class growing
outward like rings about some
blasted tree of knowledge which
somehow sends forth its yearly
shoots, though I can still make out
many of those vivid quizzing faces
by the peach-blush light of memory.

ii

From that November afternoon back
at Colgate thirty years ago, a neophyte
patting himself on the back for teaching
so crisply & deliciously on death
& dying in the work of Hemingway,
hearing the news from the car radio
outside the great gray shale stone building
that the president had been shot,
I understood there were lessons
to be learned, even on bucolic leaf-trewn
quadrangles, and that I was just then
being taught a hard one.

Or on this campus back in the spring
of '70, having left the Big Apple
for the provinces two years before,
a fresh Ph.D., a wife & three small
kids in tow, I watched as in a nightmare
as the war began spilling over into
other countries. Young men were going
under by the thousands in leech-thick
paddies, while a mad karma roiled back
on those at home. Dazed prophets
stoned on LSD & armed with bullhorns
began patrolling administration centers

that seemed to hunker down like toad
presidios. By the flare of the brave
new order one watched ghost trundles
begin rumbling across each campus.
No one over thirty could be trusted.
A girl of nineteen, flowers braiding
her fairy waistlong hair, played
a novice campus cop. "Come on,"
she kept coaxing, "let me have your
gun. That way no one will be hurt."
In the lotus-fevered milling dark
I watched as she offered him
a ring of broken daisies.

With teaching halted, there were
those who came Nicodemus-like by night
to see me. They didn't give a damn
about a grade, I was to understand, not
while this dirty little war was going on.
Unless of course the grade could be
hitched up to a B or better. Insurance,

I was made to understand, in case
the Mother of all Revolutions fizzled.

iii

That was the one side: to learn
they were only like the rest of us,
innocent, filled with delusions, less
than perfect. The other side was knowledge
stored, a honeyed wisdom gathered drop
by drop. From bouncing biases & gaucheries
off so many captive ears, even I learned
that each voice out there in the classroom
might in a single brilliant instant
reveal yet one more spoke of the great
& fiery wheel the prophets sing of.

How often too their words, reshaped
& polished, like the refurbished Hubbell
scope, opened up on galaxies of thought
I had not known till then existed.
In the give and take of the strobic
time-lapsed dance before the blackboard,
one comes to taste at last the Spirit's
gifts: wisdom, insight, reverence, patience,
heart, the knowing when to speak & when
to hold one's fire. Otherwise what one
does up there before the class becomes
mere peacock strut, the dazzling wit
which fears all difference, the small
self-interests of the tenured jackal.

iv

"If they hadn't paid me to come
and teach," the poet Randall Jarrell
wrote once, "I'd have gladly paid

to have the privilege." My sentiments
exactly, though bread being what it is,
& rent, & books, and having pored now
over ten thousand thousand papers—towers
of ivory, yes, though there were (in truth)
whole ziggurats of psychobabble too--
I'm relieved to see it work the way it has:
this being paid for what one loves to do.

"Still, you won't know until the best
of it is over what the real gifts were,"
he told me years ago, another teacher/
poet who'd seen forty years of it
in classrooms much like these,
glare-lit off-white waiting rooms
one finds in registries & morgues.
He was right, for the real payoff, once
I was smart enough to see, was what
my students taught me, though I never
told them, the story being that it was
I who'd been sent to do the teaching.

Kevin Clark

Eight Hours in the Nixon Era

The parabola of the suitcase as it flew
        from the Watergate balcony mimicked
my inner life the year the low voice
        on the phone said, FBI, do you know
a Bob Grant? My mother, a Republican

County Supervisor, was at church.
        It was a complex era. Did we laugh
too easily? Was I to tell the agent
        that Bob was a friend who'd palmed
a credit card for a wild D.C. ride

as Sam Irvin and the good guys were
        moving in for the kill? Bob, whose jet south
would pass D.C.-bound Air Force One
        that midnight, November 18th, 1973,
just after Nixon claimed he was no crook.

Bob had invited me for the gig, but
        I knew better—and I didn't know better
often. Bob seduced Ralph and Jessie,
        both staying the month in Jersey with me
and my publicity-conscious mother,

the same Ralph and Jessie who were on
        the verge of dissolution, ever since
I'd been falling for Jessie and she for me,
        though of course Ralph was my best friend,
and Jessie and I hated ourselves, hippie

clichés sloughing into a closet or basement.
          Even now I try to laugh it off. I told
Agent Kaplaw I'd never heard of Bob
          Grant. Boozy Bob, with whom I'd smoked
weed for six years in college while his muddy

Utah speakers alternately shook from
          Zeppelin sex riffs and Streisand show tunes,
who we later discovered longed himself
          to sleep with Ralph, *that* Bob had only
minutes earlier answered the suite phone,

hung up, looked at Ralph and Jessie with
          the gravity of a guy on bad acid, all
of them wordlessly putting into effect
          Escape Plan A, Ralph heading to the car
while Jessie and Bob packed the one suitcase

with the contraband of a good D.C. shopping
          blitz, compliments of a Mr. Robert Kitchen,
address at this point unknown, owner
          of a missing gold MasterCard. I hung up.
My mother pulled in the drive. The phone

didn't ring. It continued not to ring.
          As Ralph pulled to the curb and Bob and
Jessie descended down the elevator,
          exited, then stuffed the goods back
in the split suitcase and jumped into

the Cutlass, also rented courtesy of
          Mr. Kitchen, and headed for Dulles,
my mother and I chatted about Mass
          and Father Mulroney's somnambulant
sermon, though she didn't care to knock

the priest because she still harbored
        hope that my rejection of the family faith
was a temporary moral seizure and didn't
        want to sour the wine while I lapsed.
She went upstairs for her afternoon nap.

The phone rang. Agent Kaplaw assured me
        he would slap a warrant on my ass
for aiding and abetting and haul me down
        to D.C. if I didn't talk. I gave up Bob,
then hung up. Do we laugh too easily?

My mother's hero the President
        was a traitor—nothing else
she could call it. He'd lost her faith.
        And how could she win
her election next year? Car doors slammed

in front of the house. I met Ralph and Jessie
        outside. One look at me and they knew
trouble had trailed them. We called Bob
        at home in Gainesville. He would
turn himself in, as he'd promised. We

told my mother that rich Bob wasn't
        so rich as he'd made out, that he'd urged
Ralph and Jessie to DC for a weekend
        on him, that the weekend was stolen,
that the FBI had traced the billed calls

to *her* house. So practiced, we lied
        to soften the story, but
she had a Republican fit anyway.
        Soon enough Ralph left for California,
Jessie and I took a house, taught GED

in Jersey, Bob called the president
        of Mastercard and worked off
the three grand. No jail time. It's still
        a complex era, how the comic
can shroud regret. Jessie and I hit the road

for California, then broke up six years later
        when she became a Rolfer,
a Gestalt therapist, went in for enema
        and past lives therapies—
separately, I think. Bob is gay in Florida,

Ralph slept with another friend's lover,
        and now he's married to her.
I'm married, too, happy and faithful
        for two decades. In the adrenaline rush
of time, Ralph and I have remained

best of friends. We try to navigate
        all the old stories. When
our families vacation together, suitcases
        bloat, rarely fly.
I sometimes think of Nixon, how he failed us all.

Peter Balakian

Reading Dickinson/Summer '68

In the hermetic almost dark
under the fluorescent dizz

I found her broken nerves,
smoke coming off the dashes,
the caps like jolts to the neck,

the pried-open spaces between vowels
where the teeth bit off twine
and the tongue was raw then cool with ice.

The air of the stockroom after lunch
was the marbleized silence of the
small blank pages she stitched into privacy.

Air of paper and faint glue
bond, carbon, graph, yellow pads,

in the stockroom I could read alone—
the confetti of money dissolved on the blank wall.

After work, I slid the numbered poems
on blue mimeo into my playbook,
and felt the open field

the zig-zagging past cornerbacks,
the white lines skewed to heaven.

Excuse my mood—unbridled, chemical,
her scrawled messages smooth to the mind,

excuse my absence, again and yes, then, too—

the cold stone of the Palisades was there
after we split—

alone naked in the Hudson,
the water greasing me in the tepid, chemical mix,

before I returned
to the cement of 9W in my father's Skylark

the night black and soundless within.

Adrian C. Louis

San Francisco: 1969

The heartless city by the bay is
swiftly approaching a new decade.
In some cornball straight
universe Tony Bennett was crooning
his cornhole ballad but now viral
Hell had arrived in paradise:
the speed freaks, bikers, the ex-cons,
the pimps, greedy dope dealers,
the fear the CIA was tainting drugs,
the rip-off artists, narcs in the bushes
& all the lost & longing white
Indians brought him down.

So, he. . .
swallowed some Blue Cheer,
hoping to wash away the goblins
& after he started tripping saw Maya
strung out on skag levitating toward
Stanyan Street with some
greasy-dick Fillmore pimp.
She smiled at *Naatsi,* but he
couldn't, wouldn't smile at her.

Life is sacred, yet nothing is sacred.
Red eyes hid behind her dark glasses.
She looked like a sluttish vampire.

Her dead fish lips smiled faintly
at him & he didn't know
whether to shit or go blind.
His heart felt drained of blood.
His hands twitched & his balls
quivered, shriveled in his jeans.
He didn't know whether to puke or cry.
He shook his head & turned his back.
He turned his back & walked away.
Hours later, centuries, light-years later,
coming down, he found Doyle
& they made a decision to hitch east
& split from the Haight.
The love had died.
From this spot onward,
the nation is dying. . .
Sparkling psychedelic snakes
worm-danced up from the earth
& spritzed through the air.
Iridescent maggots were everywhere.
Everywhere, the love,
the love, the fucking
LOVE
had
DIED.

C.K. Williams

The Poet

I always knew him as "Bobby the poet," though whether he ever was one
     or not,
someone who lives in words, making a world from their music, might be
     a question.

In those strange years of hippiedom and "people-power," saying you were
     an artist
made you one, but at least Bobby acted the way people think poets are
     supposed to.

He dressed plainly, but with flair, spoke little, yet listened with genuine
     attention,
and a kind of preoccupied, tremulous seriousness always seemed to ab-
     sorb him.

Also he was quite good-looking, and mysterious, never saying where he'd
     come from,
nor how he lived now: I thought he might be on welfare, but you didn't
     ask that.

He'd been around town for a while, had dropped from sight for a few
     months when
one evening he came up to me in the local bookstore; I could see he
     hadn't been well.

He looked thin, had a soiled sling tied on one arm, the beret he usually
     wore was gone,
and when I turned to him he edged back like a child who's afraid you
     might hit him.

He smiled at himself then, but without humor; his eyes were partly
        closed, from dope,
I guessed, then changed my mind: this seemed less arbitrary, more pur-
        poseful.

Still, he had to tilt his head back a little to keep me in focus in his field
        of vision:
it was disconcerting, I felt he was looking at me from a place far away in
        himself.

"Where've you been, Bobby?" I asked. He didn't answer at first, but
        when I asked again,
he whispered, "In the hospital, man; I had a breakdown . . . they took me
        away there."

Then he subsided into his smile, and his silence. "What happened to
        your arm?"
He dipped his shoulder, his sling opened, and cradled along his arm was
        a long knife.

"That looks dangerous," I said; "I need it," he came back with, and the
        sling came closed.
I was startled. Did he think someone was out to hurt him? Might he
        think it was me?

He never stopped looking at me: his agitation was apparent and not re-
        assuring;
we'd been friendly, but I didn't know him that well. "Where's your
        book?" I asked finally.

He'd always carried an old-fashioned bound accountant's ledger, its
        pages scrawled
with columns of poems: his "book," though as far as I knew no one but
        he ever read it.

Again no response; I remember the store was well-lit, but my image of
        him is shadow;
the light seemed extracted from his presence, obliterated by the mass of
        his anguish.

Poets try to help one another when we can: however competitive we are,
        and we are,
the life's so chancy, we feel so beleaguered, we need all the good will we
        can get.

Whether you're up from a slum or down from a carriage, how be sure
        you're a poet?
How know if your work has enduring worth, or any? Self-doubt is almost
        our definition.

Now, waiting with Bobby, I could tell he'd had enough of all that, he
        wanted out;
that may have explained his breakdown, but what was it he expected
        from me?

I was hardly the most visible poet around; I'd published little, didn't give
        readings,
or teach, although, come to think of it, maybe that's just what Bobby was
        after.

Someone once said that to make a poem, you first have to invent the
        poet to make it:
Bobby'd have known I'd understand how the first person he'd devised
        had betrayed him.

Bobby, from nowhere, Bobby know-nothing, probably talentless Bobby:
        wasn't that me?
I'd know as well as he did how absurd it could be to take your trivial self
        as the case.

But if Bobby'd renounced poetry, what was my part to be? To acknowl-
   edge it for him?
Flatter him? Tell him to keep on? I might well have, but not without
   knowing his work.

Then it came to me that his being here meant more than all that—it was
   a challenge;
Bobby wanted to defy me, and whatever he'd taken into his mind I rep-
   resented.

The truth is I was flattered myself, that it was me he'd chosen, but there
   was that knife.
Though the blade was thin, serrated, to cut bread, not tendon or bone, it
   still was a knife.

It could hurt you: despite myself, I felt my eyes fall to its sorry scabbard,
   and as I did,
I could see Bobby'd caught my concern: he seemed to come to attention,
   to harden.

Though he still hadn't threatened me quite—he never did—I knew now
   I was afraid,
and Bobby did, too: I could sense his exaltation at having so invaded my
   emotions;

an energy all at once emanated from him, a quaver, of satisfaction, or an-
   ticipation:
"This is my poem," he might have been saying, "are you sure yours are
   worth more?"

Then the moment had passed; it was as though Bobby had flinched,
   though he hadn't,
torn his gaze from mine, though it clung, but we both knew now nothing
   would happen,

we both realized Bobby's menace was a mask, that it couldn't conceal his
       delicacy,
the gentle sensitivity that would have been so useful if he'd been able to
       keep writing.

He must have felt me thinking that, too; something in him shut down,
       and I wondered:
would he take this as a defeat? Whose, though? And what would a vic-
       tory have been?

He turned then and without a word left, leaving me stranded there with
       my books
while he drifted out into the rest of his life, weighed down with his evasions,
       and mine.

I never found out what he came to in the end; I've always kept him as
       "Bobby the poet."
I only hope he didn't suffer more rue, that the Muse kept watch on her
       innocent stray.

Adrian C. Louis

April 24, 1971

It's his birthday
& he's twenty-five
on the lawn in DC
near the Lincoln Memorial
getting a wicked hand job
from some white girl he just met.
There's lots of people around.
Maybe 500,000 humans.
They're protesting Vietnam.
FIVE HUNDRED THOUSAND
American sexual organs!
He shoots his load shortly
before the tear gas cannons
begin their first bombardment.
Maybe the revolution has started
but *Naatsi* no longer cares.
The '60s are over &
he's tired of scenes.
The '60s are over
& the future looks
mind-dead & televised,
grim, greedy & goofy.

Robert Phillips

The Death of Janis Joplin

"Oh, Lord, won't you buy me a Mercedes-Benz!..."
October 4, 1970

Because she was a white girl
      born black-and-blue,
because she was outsized victim
      of her own insides,
because she was voted
      "Ugliest Man on Campus,"
because she looked for something
      and found nothing—
      she became famous.

"Tell me that you love me!"
      she screamed at audiences.
They told. Fat Janis wouldn't
      believe. Twenty-seven,
a star since twenty-four,
      she tried to suck, lick,
smoke, shoot, drip, drop,
      drink the world.
      Nothing worked.

Bought a house, a place
      to go home to.
Bought a dog, something to give
      love to. Nothing worked.
Jimi Hendrix died, Janis cried:
      "Goddamn. He beat me

to it!" Not by much. Three weeks
later she joined him.
Part of something at last.

Janet Lowery

The *Dharma Kia* Foundation

Just before he left for the Zen Center in Rochester,
Eliot had business cards printed for our communal
farmhouse at 2955 Lake Road, phone number
703-637-3995, the words *call collect anytime*
in small italicized print under the number,
the farm's karmic name in the center:
The Dharma Kia Foundation.
No one we didn't know ever called collect—
thank God, Yahweh, Jesus, Allah, Buddha,
Krishna, Shiva-Shakti, Zeus, Odin
and the One Lao-tsu knew so much about—
because we were all broke.

This was the early seventies and we covered
all the bases when we referred to Source,
we chanted *om* over every meal, repeating
o-shree-ram-jaa-ram, jaa-jaa ram when we meditated
in the sloping country house I considered a palace,
but which my father refused to enter the one time
he visited me in the alternate community.

A group of vegetarian students, we lived
in an off-shoot collective from the Armadillo Ranch,
so named by Texas stage director Arnie Kendall
and his ballerina wife, Judy, when they lived
for a short time in upstate New York.
After they and their original crew of former
students and artist friends had saved enough money,

they bought a hundred-acre farm in West Virginia,
quit their academic jobs and headed south.

Whereas we, the second generation of young
artists, poets, musicians, and dancers, we went ahead
and created the first food co-op in our college town.
Friday night we collected orders for fruits, vegetables,
nuts, grains, cheeses, spices, and oils, sold in bulk
at the local farmers' market in the big city,
then jump-started Stan's VW bug every Saturday
at 6:00 a.m. to drive into Rochester, haggling
with vendors for the pretty fruit.

We bought a contraband radionics machine
from England, used a pendulum and a lock of hair
to find out what was ailing us—illegal in the US
then and now except to use on animals because
it works and it's cheap and easy to use. We planted
huge gardens, built saunas, bought a milk goat
and milked it every morning, despite that kicking hind leg.
We played guitars and fiddles and harmonicas
and bongos every night, singing Dylan, Guthrie,
Baez and old blues tunes with some Hank Williams
thrown in for good measure.

Stan walked around naked most days, but no one
much noticed or cared. We were drug- and alcohol-
free, and people who visited us from town
said we were more highly evolved—the way
we prayed and sang and ate, we were moving
things along by example and it was true
that we loved each other and trusted each other,
we laughed together, built fires in the stove
in the winters, planted in the spring, weeded

in the summer, ground our own flour, sprouted
our own seeds, played pick-up basketball games
and games of catch, practiced giving massages,
we traveled across country in VW vans,
jump-starting them every other day,

or we hitchhiked—even us girls—risking our lives
to be like Jack Kerouac, getting raped
by truckers in the northeast corridor only,
whereas those in the South, Midwest,
and on the West Coast protected us, but that was
the price we paid to travel like the guys,
we picked ourselves up and dusted ourselves off,
everything being karma, including sexual trauma,
karma, karma, karma until we broke that spell
too and evolved beyond those narrow limits
to rejoin humanity, a message of freedom
and reverence cultivated like a little garden
in our heart chakras, spinning its wheel,
our souls spinning farther down the beautiful roads,
the lonely highways and lovely byways
of this gravity-bound plane we never want to leave. . .

Jim Daniels

Shedding the Sixties

I slept with a high percentage of my friends.
Intuited randomness—sex to clarify
and muddle. My housemates and I surprised
each other in the morning, seeing who
walked through door #2. We specialized
in cooking big pots full of whatever
and eating it for a week—stew, soup, chili.
Bringing your acoustic guitar
to a party wasn't considered quaint
and candles were taken seriously.
We patiently took off each other's jeans,
imagining we had forever. My old dog
slept through it all, constantly shedding.
Once a month we borrowed a vacuum cleaner.
Of course, he's dead now.

Stephen Dunn

The Sexual Revolution

In that time of great freedom to touch
        and get in touch,
we lived on the prairie amid polite

moral certainty. The sensate world seemed
        elsewhere, and was.
On our color television the president's body

admitted he was lying. There was marching
        in the suddenly charged streets,
and what a girl in a headband and miniskirt

called *communication*. A faraway friend wrote
        to say the erotic life
was the only life. Get with it, he said.

But many must have been slow-witted
        during The Age of Enlightenment,
led artless lives during The Golden Age.

We watched the revolution on the evening news.
        It was 1972
when the sixties reached all the way

to where we were. The air became alive
        with incense and license.
The stores sold permission and I bought

and my wife bought until we were left
            with almost nothing.
Even the prairie itself changed;

people began to call it the Land, and once again
            it was impossibly green
and stretched endlessly ahead of us.

David Lehman

Paris, 1971

In retrospect it was romantic to be the lonely American recovering from pneumonia living in a hotel room with a typewriter and a sink in a Left Bank Hotel in a gray Paris winter.

At the time I was constantly cold, it rained seven days a week, my feet were wet, I was awkward with girls and wanted sex so badly I couldn't sleep at night, in London.

In retrospect I was neither Alyosha nor Ivan, not Orwell in Spain nor Hemingway on a fishing trip nor Henry Miller in Clichy.

At the time I saw *The Wild Bunch*, Sergio Leone's *Duck, You Sucker, The Go-Between, Sunday, Bloody Sunday,* and *Woodstock.*

In retrospect the gloom of the deserted streets and the sound of footfalls were full of strangeness in medieval Cambridge.

At the time I became self-conscious about my American accent. I began pronouncing the t's in words like "city" or "university," and I said tomah-to at the greengrocer's.

In retrospect I spent more money than my friends did at restaurants like the Koh-I-Noor, the Gardenia on Rose Crescent, and the Rembrandt. Then I learned to cook.

At the time I was in London for the weekend. There was a new place called the Great American Disaster that specialized in hamburgers. I saw John Gielgud in a matinee.

In retrospect I met a Swedish woman named Eva, blonde and beautiful, and the sex was great but we had nothing to talk about and I grew melancholy in the Scandinavian manner.

At the time I moved into an apartment near the rue des Écoles with a dandy who had a magnificent cane and liked walking with me to Montparnasse where a couple of Chaplin films were showing.

In retrospect I read "Le Cimetière marin" by Paul Valéry.

At the time I was a naive American in a trench coat and fedora trying to make ends meet in Berlin in the waning days of the Weimar Republic.

In retrospect Beckett and Lorca. At the time Stravinsky and Frank Zappa.

In retrospect Otto Dix, Andre Dérain, and the Ballets suédois.

At the time the Pompes Funébres sign between Saint Sulpice and Saint Placide.

In retrospect we spent hours in the Rond-Point café playing Dipsy Doodle and other pinball machines made by the U.S. manufacturer Williams.

At the time steak tartare with capers and cornichons at Le Drugstore. I was sick for two days after.

In retrospect we went to Le Dôme, La Rotonde, Le Select, La Coupole, and the best of these was Le Dôme.

At the time Nicole was waiting to find out whether she could come to England to have an abortion. She was my friend, not my girlfriend, I wasn't responsible.

In retrospect, the English doctor gave me as dirty a look as I've ever faced.

At the time of the Ali-Frazier fight at the Garden a smell like that of peaches wafted in the air, and spring was only weeks away.

In retrospect the Opéra, the Madeleine, the Sainte Chapelle, the Sacré Coeur, the Saint Germain.

At the time the Jockey Club where Lew played the piano and we cheered him on—Gail and I and Tim and maybe even Edda.

In retrospect I visited Paul Auster in a garret near the Louvre, which he got with the help of Jacques Dupin.

At the time I read Simenon in French and (on Auster's recommendation) *The Real Life of Sebastian Knight*. He gave me a copy of his poem "Stele," and Larry Joseph filched it.

In retrospect I began a poem entitled "Interrupted Messages" and left it on my desk. Jonathan Lear came by when I wasn't in and wrote a note on the poem ending in the hope that he hadn't "sullied a vital piece of paper." I liked "sullied."

At the time the blue airmail letter summoning me to my father's deathbed arrived on a Tuesday morning. The in-flight movie on the way home was *Love Story*. I didn't see it. The off-duty flight attendant sitting next to me was engaged to be married to a minor league shortstop from Broken Arrow, Oklahoma.

In retrospect I took French lessons at the Alliance Française and went with a Spanish girl to a movie with Jean Gabin and Simone Signoret as an old quarrelsome married couple.

At the time I watched the little kids sail their toy boats in the Jardin du Luxembourg.

In retrospect I was always alone.

At the time I sat with you in the Bois de Boulogne and we took turns guessing what was in the mind of each person passing by.

Stanley Plumly

Four Hundred Mourners

The sizes of the crowds in those burn-baby-burn days
were at best estimates, depending on who—
the police, the press, the thousands in protest—
was counting. The body count, we called it,
and after the arrest we were lined up
alphabetically for fingerprints and phone calls.
It wasn't all that much, though the numbers
made a difference since they argued significance.
That was later, at the dead end of the sixties,
the rallies against the war mixed with the killings
of the Kennedys and King and the nuclear meltdown
of democracy at the convention in Chicago.
But at the beginning of the decade
it was man-on-the-moon, hand-on-the-heart.
Ralph Abernathy, who had recruited most of us,
came by one day just to say hello.
We were on the white side of the table,
the soon-to-be-eligible black voters on the other.
Greenville was as liberal as it got in Mississippi,
the Delta almost as ancient as the flooding of the Nile.
The names, the spellings, the signatures,
like maps of a world once flat.
And the heat and the dog's-breath weight of the air
and the wet dust needlework of pine.
People had died here under a different register,
as thousands more thousands of nautical miles
southeast would die who had not voted.
Ralph said the numbers finally didn't matter,
the idea of change was enough.

He meant "an idea whose time has come."
The few new voters each seemed wise and old,
older than anyone we knew, older than parents
or grandparents, older than the country
or anger's life expectancy.
They had looked into the sun,
they had looked into it a long time.
The Carter family newspaper spoke of joy
with sometimes grief, as if the happiness
of change felt like a passage.
This is fifty years now, gone.
It's crazy that so much of it came back to me
witnessing the funeral of a child.
The countless car cortege wound through the town's
winter wastes as if the hearse could not quite find its
       way.
There is no end to the death of a child,
so that when we detoured past her elementary school
everyone was out in the cold, in the hundreds, waving.

Stephen Dunn

Around the Time of the Moon

The experts were at work doing expert work.
Amateurs were loving what they hardly knew.
Houston, Tranquility Base here, the Eagle
has landed—came over our televisions,
accidental poetry, instant lore.
Our parents couldn't believe it.
Can you believe it? said my sister Sam.
Elsewhere on terra firma, a chemist
must have smiled an inner smile,
perfected Agent Orange.
A guy on acid said he was the bullet,
but sometimes also the wound.
The moon was finished, he went on to explain,
never again would haunt or beguile.
Mary Travers was leaving on a jet plane,
didn't know when she'd be back again;
I, for one, was sad. During the day
quotation marks descended from the sky,
fit around everything we thought we knew.
And under artificial light in our rooms,
we read strangely comforting books
about alienation and despair.
Soon everyone had a harmonica.
On every street corner, a guitar.
Many of us were love's amateurs,
its happy fools. The obstinate moon,
meanwhile, trod upon or not, kept bumping
up the crime rate, lifting the helpless seas.

Jim Elledge

"Their Hats is Always White"

Just an hour before the hump of last night, when—not
with an old-fashioned ringing but high-tech, high-
pitched trills—the phone slit ear to ear the throat of his
latest, best dream (How easily dinosaurs—big ones!—
plopped to their knees when his whizzing club plunked
against their heads. How light the woman's body—a big
one!—grew, her hair coiling up his wrist.), he leapt up out
of bed, untangling from lasso blankets, more naked than
breath #1 to answer a dial tone.

Oops! Not his. The lady's next door. Their common wall a
bulletin board of cigarette hacking, coo-coo clock chirps,
bedspring wheezes.

Like a radio shrink on the graveyard shift reciting
parables in kilowatts until cock-crow, her voice clawed at
plaster, drawing blood.

"I saw Elvis today," she said. She said, "At the Washing
Well." "Pulled up in a black, stretch Caddy spit-shined,"
she said. She said, "White jump suits tumble-drying
in the cut-est little tango." "He said Vegas was A-OK
and tell ever'body he luvs 'em, specially them stayed fans
through thick an' thin," she said. She said, "Just needed
a vacation. That's all." "Wrote 'To Lola from The King'
in magic marker on them happy face bikinis Ronny Lee
gave me last Valentine's Day," said. Said, "I was tossin' no-
static strips into dryers, and whoosh, he vanished in thin
air." "Thought I'd died and gone to my reward," she said.

Light filled the tabby's water dish and the kitchen sink, dusted the dining room table and TV screen, fell onto the Persian carpet in game-board squares.

Outside, a flying saucer hovered about to land. A blink later, no: a full moon rounded through clouds that got clean away.

Michael Waters

Sixties Sonnet

I have become handsome in my old age.

"You're cute," smiled Denise, breaking up with me,
"But cute is all you'll ever be."

Denise who was so wrongwrongwrong, I miss
Our Woodstock nights, half-a-million thumb-flicked

Bics coaxed to climax by God's thwapping bass,
Hissing soppy Oms against the cloudmass.

A drenched, naked hillside soulless and pure,
Zonked, mud-caked, Yanomamö, immature.

I forgive Sly and the Family Stone.
I slept through Santana, dreaming future

Exes who might love me despite my rage.
I have grown lonesome in my afflictions.

I have become handsome in my old age.

Martín Espada

The Year I Was Diagnosed
With a Sacrilegious Heart

At twelve, I quit reciting
the Pledge of Allegiance,
could not salute the flag
in 1969, and I,
undecorated for grades or sports,
was never again anonymous in school.

A girl in homeroom
caught my delinquent hand
and pinned a salute
against my chest;
my cafeteria name was Commie,
though I too drank the milk
with presidential portraits on the carton;
but when the school assembly stood
for the flags and stiff soldiers' choreography
of the color guard,
and I stuck to my seat
like a back pocket snagged on coil,
the principal's office
quickly found my file.
A balding man in a brown suit
asked me if I understood compromise,
and we nodded in compromise,
a pair of Brooklyn wardheelers.

Next assembly, when the color guard
marched down the aisle,

stern-faced,
I stood with the rest,
then pivoted up the aisle,
the flags and me
brushing past each other
without apologies,
my unlaced sneakers
dragging out of the auditorium.

I pressed my spyglass eye
against the doors
for the Pledge:
no one saw my right hand
crumpled in a pocket
instead of spreading
across my sacrilegious heart.

Ceremony done, the flagpoles
pointed their eagle beaks at me,
and I ducked
under their drifting banner wings
back to my seat,
inoculated against staring,
my mind a room after school
where baseball cards
could be stacked by team
in a plastic locker.

Janet McCann

In Front of the Coke Machine

A silver quarter in my change! I am blessed.
It radiates in my palm, a shiny disk,
George Washington's pure face.
For three flights up I gaze at it in awe.
I drop it on my desk and it rings true.

1964. Where has it been for more than
forty years? In some forgotten pocket,
a jewelry box, the drawer of an old desk?
Perhaps it's been around, though it looks new,
fresh-minted yesterday and stamped for me.

In sixty-four I ran free in sandals,
smoked grass in two-room apartments, drank Georgia Moon
from Dixie cups, stayed up nights reading Proust.
In sixty-four I wrote poems about God,
debated Kierkegaard, marched through cities,

ate fifteen tacos for second prize, did cartwheels
on the Capitol lawn, occupied the
locked faculty john, was arrested twice
for trespassing, and everything was silver, silver
and rang true.

Wendy Barker

Miniskirts

How short was short? Trying them on at Julie's mom and
dad's dress shop in the Marina, I wanted them as high as
I could get but not show the bottom curve of my buns. At
least when I was standing up.

That was three years before Julie killed herself, Julie who
knew without question her boobs were her best attribute,
who wouldn't lose weight, carried a little extra because if
she dropped even a couple of pounds, they shrank. One
of the P.E. teachers, which one was it, said Julie had a big
sloppy pussy, really liked to be gone down on, but in the
end, after she'd been found dead with the principal's baby
inside her—someone said he'd refused to divorce his wife
in Oakland, and Julie had wanted to get married and have
his baby no matter how black—in the end, it turned out it
was the girls' track coach, Louise, who'd wanted her most,
and Julie couldn't decide. By then I was long gone. Earth
shoes, corduroys, no makeup. Hell with it. Just do what
you gotta do, get on with it.

Robert Bly

Driving West in 1970

My dear children, do you remember the morning
We climbed into the old Plymouth
And drove west straight toward the Pacific?

We were all the people there were.
We followed Dylan's songs all the way west.
It was Seventy; the war was over, almost;

And we were driving to the sea.
We had closed the farm, tucked in
The flap, and were eating the honey

Of distance and the word "there."
Oh whee, we're gonna fly
Down in the easy chair. We sang that

Over and over. That's what the early
Seventies were like. We weren't afraid.
A hole had opened in the world.

We laughed at Las Vegas.
There was enough gaiety
For all of us, and ahead of us

Was the ocean. *Tomorrow's*
The day my bride's gonna come.
And the war was over, almost.

ABOUT THE POETS

Ai was born in Albany, Texas, in 1947 and grew up in Tucson. She also lived in Las Vegas and San Francisco. Describing herself as half Japanese, Choctaw-Chickasaw, Black Irish, Southern Cheyenne, and Comanche, she renamed herself "Ai" which means "love" in Japanese. She held an M.F.A. from the University of California at Irvine. She was the author of *Dread* (W.W. Norton & Co., 2003); *Vice: New and Selected Poems* (W.W. Norton & Co., 1999), which won the National Book Award, *Greed* (W.W. Norton & Co., 1993), *Fate* (Houghton Mifflin, 1991), *Sin* (Houghton Mifflin, 1986), which won an American Book Award from the Before Columbus Foundation, *Killing Floor* (Houghton Mifflin, 1979), which was the 1978 Lamont Poetry Selection of the Academy of American Poets, and *Cruelty* (Perseus Books Group, 1973). She received awards from the Guggenheim Foundation, the NEA, and the Bunting Fellowship Program at Radcliffe College. She died in 2010.

Robert Alexander grew up in Massachusetts. He attended the University of Wisconsin and for several years taught in the Madison public schools. After receiving his Ph.D. from the University of Wisconsin–Milwaukee, he worked as a freelance editor. From 1993-2001, he was a contributing editor at New Rivers Press, also serving from 1999-2001 as New Rivers' creative director. Alexander has published two books of poetry, a book of creative nonfiction about the American Civil War, and has edited or co-edited five literary anthologies. He is the founding editor of the Marie Alexander Poetry Series at White Pine Press. His website: www.robertalexander.info.

About the '60s: At the beginning of the '60s, I was in seventh grade, living in Brookline, Massachusetts, just a mile or so from Fenway Park. My father worked at the Beth Israel hospital, and during the summer we'd walk over to Fenway to see the Red Sox play an afternoon game. Later in the decade I began to listen to jazz. Some of my fondest memories stem from weekends I spent visiting my girlfriend at NYU. One club in stands out in my mind, Slugs' on the Lower East Side, which was later closed down after a murder took place there.

Michael Anania is a poet, essayist, and fiction writer. His published work includes twelve collections of poetry, among them *Selected Poems* (1994), *In Natural Light* (1999), *Once Again, Flowered* (2001), and *Heat Lines* (2006). His newest collection is *Continuous Showings (* 2015). His poetry is widely anthologized and has been translated into Italian, German, French, Spanish, and Czech. He also published a novel, *The Red Menace,* and a collection of essays, *In Plain Sight.* Anania was poetry editor of *Audit,* a quarterly, founder and co-editor of *Audit/Poetry,* poetry editor of *Partisan Review,* a contributing editor to *Tri-Quarterly* and poetry and literary editor of The Swallow Press. He also served as a panelist for the NEA, the NEH, and the Illinois Arts Council. Anania has taught at SUNY at Buffalo, Northwestern University and the University of Chicago and is Professor Emeritus of English at the University of Illinois at Chicago. He lives in Austin, Texas, and on Lake Michigan.

About the '60s: I spent the '60s, the actual decade, in Omaha, in Buffalo and in Chicago. I spent the mythic '60s, which started in 1965 and lasted into the '70s, teaching at Northwestern and the University of Illinois at Chicago and editing. During the Vietnam War there was a television program called the *Vietnam Week in Review,* with Frank Reynolds, I think. That's where I saw interview quoted in the poem.

Judith Arcana writes poems, stories, essays and books. Her books include *Grace Paley's Life Stories, A Literary Biography;* the poetry collection *What if your mother;* and the poetry chapbook *4th Period English.* Judith's most recent publications are a chapbook of poems, *The Parachute Jump Effect* (2012); a prose fiction zine, *Keesha and Joanie and JANE* (2013); and a set of three broadsides, *The Water Portfolio* (2014). Her Maude poems, a project supported by grants from both NW Oregon's Regional Arts and Culture Council and The Celebration Foundation, are part of a book manuscript now seeking publication—as are her JANE stories, a linked fiction collection. Additionally (and wonderfully), a sandwich was recently named for her at the lovely & amazing Fleur De Lis bakery/café in Portland. You can listen to Judith read poetry on SoundCloud (https://soundcloud.com/judith-arcana) and tell a story at KBOO (http://

kboo.fm/content/bearwitnessjuditharcana); for more info and
links, visit http://www.juditharcana.com/

About the '60s: From 1960 to 1964 I was a student
at three colleges in Illinois; I graduated from one of them,
Northwestern University. From 1964 to 1970, I was a high
school teacher in Niles Township, Illinois (English, Humani-
ties, Creative Writing). In both situations, especially the latter,
I was becoming conscious; like so many in that decade, I was
learning from the courage and intelligence of the civil rights
movement, which fostered the fiercely idealistic anti-war and
women's liberation movements. Because of what I'd been learn-
ing, the decade ended with two changes for me: I was fired
from my tenured teaching position in March of 1970, accused
of unorthodox methods and dangerously radical attitudes; six
months later, in October, I joined an underground abortion
service, a group now commonly called JANE, to help thousands
of women and girls get safe illegal abortions.

Peter Balakian is the author of seven books of poems, most
recently *Ozone Journal* (University of Chicago, 2015). His other
books include: *Vise and Shadow: Selected Essays on the Lyrical
Imagination, Poetry, Art, and Culture* (University of Chicago,
2015), *Black Dog of Fate*, winner of the PEN/Alband Prize for
memoir, and *The Burning Tigris: The Armenian Genocide and
America's Response* , which was a New York Times best seller
and winner of the Raphael Lemkin Prize. He directs Creative
Writing at Colgate.

About the '60s: In 1968 I was a pretty traditional subur-
ban high school kid in Tenafly and Englewood, New Jersey—a
running back and co-captain of the football team. On the
outside I was part of an affluent suburban world of girl friends,
parties, proms, and pranks. On the inside other things were
going on, and reading Emily Dickinson, among others, in
the *Mentor Book of Major Poets*, edited by Oscar Williams and
Edwin Honig was part of my inner life. That anthology—an
old-fashioned pre-trade paperback that cost a buck fifty, the
paper almost as cheap as newspaper—carried all those poems—
from Edward Taylor to Auden. I'm grateful to my 11th grade
high school English teacher Mike Hechmer for sending that
book our way.

Rebecca Balcárcel's first book, *Palabras in Each Fist*, was released by Pecan Grove Press in 2010. Her work has appeared in over forty journals, such as *North American Review, Segue, Oklahoma Review, descant,* and *Third Coast.* She serves the students of Tarrant County College as Associate Professor of English and enjoys giving readings at libraries and schools. She regularly presents at conferences as well. A native of Iowa, Rebecca Balcárcel moved to Texas in 1980 with her Guatemalan dad and Anglo mom. Fun facts: she has skydived, nursed twins, and biked from Houston to Santa Fe.

About the '60s: In a time when Ricky Ricardo "esplained" things to Lucy, and Lawrence Welk sashayed to "Down Mexico Way," my father, a Guatemalan, emigrated to the United States. Seen as a novelty in the college town of Le Mars, Iowa, Federico Balcárcel made friends with everyone from meat packing workers to professors. He'd left behind country and family to marry a Peace Corps volunteer, a woman who'd heard President Kennedy's call to service on television and signed up. This poem celebrates his experience.

Wendy Barker's sixth collection of poetry, *One Blackbird at a Time* (BkMk Press, 2015), received the John Ciardi Prize for Poetry. Her fourth chapbook is *From the Moon, Earth Is Blue* (Wings Press, 2015). Other books include a selection of poems with accompanying essays, *Poems' Progress* (Absey & Co., 2002), and a selection of translations, *Rabindranath Tagore: Final Poems* (co-translated with Saranindranath Tagore, Braziller, 2001). Her poems have appeared in numerous journals (including *The Southern Review, Poetry, The Gettysburg Review, Mid-American Review, Georgia Review,* and *Southern Poetry Review*) and in many anthologies, including *The Best American Poetry 2013.* She is poetry editor of *Persimmon Tree: An Online Journal of the Arts for Women Over Sixty.* Recipient of NEA and Rockefeller fellowships among other awards, she is Poet-in-Residence and the Pearl LeWinn Endowed Professor of Creative Writing at the University of Texas at San Antonio. Her website is http://wendybarker.net/.

About the '60s: Having turned 20 in 1962, I'd dropped out of college to marry, and, with my husband, moved to Tombstone, Arizona where he taught music and I worked as secretary to the Superintendent of Schools. In 1964 I enrolled at A.S.U., where I finished my B.A. In 1966 I taught at Scottsdale's Saguaro High, and then, between 1968-1972, in West Berkeley, during the implementation of the Berkeley Public Schools' all-city integration plan. Barely ten years older than my students, I was caught in the maelstrom of all the interracial, political, and other cultural whirlwinds sweeping the Bay Area during those years. The poems included here are taken from *Nothing Between Us: The Berkeley Years*, a "novel" in prose poems reflecting on my experiences as young, white, and married, I struggled to teach ninth graders in a school located in a primarily black neighborhood a few blocks from the newly formed Black Panthers headquarters.

Aliki Barnstone is a poet, translator, critic, editor, and visual artist. She is the author of eight volumes of poetry, most recently *Dear God Dear, Dr. Heartbreak: New and Selected Poems* (Sheep Meadow, 2009), *Bright Body* (White Pine, 2011), and a chapbook, *Winter, with Child* (Red Dragonfly Press, 2015). She is the translator of *The Collected Poems of C.P. Cavafy* (W.W. Norton, 2006). Her first book of poems, *The Real Tin Flower* (Crowell-Collier, 1968), was published when she was 12 years old, with an introduction by Anne Sexton. In 2014, her book, *Madly in Love,* was reissued as a Carnegie-Mellon Classic Contemporary. She has edited two anthologies of women's poetry. Her literary critical work includes an edition of H.D.'s *Trilogy* and *Changing Rapture: The Development of Emily Dickinson's Poetry* (UPNE, 2007). Among her awards is a Fulbright Fellowship in Greece. She is Professor of English at the University of Missouri.

About the '60s: During the '60s I went to elementary school in Bloomington, Indiana, and spent summers in Vermont. My mother, Elli, a painter, didn't allow any TV or phone, and she freed me and my brothers, Robert and Tony, to spend our summers for walking mountaintop fields, swimming cold lakes, writing, painting, playing checkers and chess, and reading. We lived near Ruth Stone and her daughters, Marcia, Phoebe, and Abigail. Abigail and I were in love with the Beatles and watched them on the Ed Sullivan show. Our families would gather around Ruth's fireplace, eat a spaghetti dinner, roast marshmallows, and play the poetry game. The Vietnam War escalated and my parents opposed it. My dad, Willis, took students from Indiana to the Pentagon March. Young Back-to-the-Landers found refuge in Vermont. Raised with these models, I was a feminist, social-justice-and-peace-activist, and environmentalist from the start.

Chana Bloch's *Swimming in the Rain: New and Selected Poems, 1980-2015,* begins with new work and includes selections from her four earlier collections, *The Secrets of the Tribe, The Past Keeps Changing, Mrs. Dumpty,* and *Blood Honey.* Bloch is co-translator of the biblical *Song of Songs* and of Israeli poets Yehuda Amichai and Dahlia Ravikovitch. Among her honors are two Pushcart Prizes, two NEA fellowships, the Felix Pollak Prize in Poetry, the Di Castagnola Award of the Poetry Society of America, and the PEN Award for Poetry in Translation, as well as multiple residencies at Yaddo, MacDowell, Djerassi, and Bellagio. Bloch is Professor Emerita of English at Mills College, where she directed the Creative Writing Program. She was the first Poetry Editor of *Persimmon Tree: An Online Journal Of the Arts By Women Over Sixty.*

About the '60s: In the early '60s I studied at Cornell (BA, English Lit) and Brandeis (MAs, Near Eastern & Judaic Studies and English). I taught English and studied Yiddish at the Hebrew University in Jerusalem in 1964-67. From my balcony I could hear the mortar shells whizzing by in the 1967 war; I believed (naïvely) that peace would follow quickly. In 1967 I moved to Berkeley, teaching Biblical Hebrew and studying for my PhD in English at the University of California. I fell in love with Berkeley and everything I missed when abroad— the latest slang, the Beatles, feminism, and politics.

Robert Bly has published over thirty books of poems and translations. He was active in the anti-war movement of the 1960s and contributed his National Book Award prize money for his collection *The Light Around the Body* to the War Resisters League. Bly remains one of the most hotly debated American artists of the past half-century. The Jungian psychologist Robert Moore has said, "When the cultural and intellectual history of our time is written, Robert Bly will be recognized as the catalyst for a sweeping cultural revolution." Bly's most recent books of poems include *Stealing Sugar from the Castle: New and Selected Poems* (W. W. Norton) and *Like the New Moon I Will Live My Life* (White Pine). His correspondence with Tomas Tranströmer was published recently as *Airmail: The Letters of Robert Bly and Tomas Tranströmer* (Graywolf Press). He lives in Minneapolis with his wife Ruth.

Robert Bonazzi was born in New York City in 1942, and has lived in San Francisco, Mexico City, Florida and several Texas cities. He is the author of five collections of poetry, the most recent being *The Scribbling Cure: Poems & Prose Poems* (Pecan Grove, 2012). "Like all good art," wrote *Way Magazine*, "Bonazzi's lucid poems become a weapon against whatever profaning spirit says that truth is only a matter of opinion." From 1966 until 2000, he edited and published over one hundred titles under his Latitudes Press imprint. Bonazzi is the author of the critically-acclaimed *Man in the Mirror: John Howard Griffin and the Story of Black Like Me* (Orbis Books, 1997, 2003). He recently completed a decade-long project, the authorized biography of John Howard Griffin, to be entitled *Reluctant Activist.* A collection of literary commentaries, *Outside the Margins,* was published by Wings Press in 2015.

    About the '60s: During the 1960s, I was a student in English at the University of Houston, then a graduate teaching fellow, and finally taught at a local high school that was being integrated. After two years there, I moved in 1968 to New York, my birthplace. This poem was written that year, influenced by the poetry of Peruvian César Vallejo, who had been championed in the pages of Robert Bly's *The Sixties.* The poem was published in *The New York Times* (when it printed poems on the editorial page during the years I taught high school English in Brooklyn). Later it appeared in my first book, *Living the Borrowed Life* from New Rivers Press in 1974.

Fleda Brown's eighth collection of poems, *No Need for Sympathy* (BOA Editions, LTD), and her collection of essays, with Vermont Poet Laureate Sydney Lea, *Growing Old in Poetry:*

Two Poets, Two Lives (Autumn House Books), came out in 2013. Her memoir is *Driving with Dvorak* (University of Nebraska Press, 2010). Fleda's work has appeared in *Best American Poetry*, has won a Pushcart Prize, the Felix Pollak Prize, the Philip Levine Prize, and the Great Lakes Colleges New Writer's Award. She has won the *New Letters* and the Ohio State Univ/*The Journal* awards for creative nonfiction. She is professor emerita at the University of Delaware, where she taught for 27 years and directed the Poets in the Schools program. She was poet laureate of Delaware from 2001-07. She and her husband, Jerry Beasley, now live in Traverse City, Michigan.

     About the '60s: I was an undergraduate at the University of Arkansas in Fayetteville, a hotbed of radicalism. On Dickson Street at George's Lounge, you could get professional anti-draft counseling 24 a day. A group of creative writing faculty climbed the giant pine tree in front of the student union, nude, to protest the war. An "underground" paper, "The Grapevine," started up by hippies and graduate students (I think my first poem publication was there, an Anne Sexton knockoff). What was I doing? I was married. I was having babies, changing diapers, studying in the time in between. I left school, then returned. All the turmoil of the '60s took place only in my peripheral vision.

W. E. Butts (1944-2013), New Hampshire Poet Laureate 2009-2014, was the author of several poetry collections, including *Sunday Evening at the Stardust Café*, winner of the 2006 Iowa Source Poetry Book Prize and a finalist for the Philip Levine Prize in Poetry from the University of California at Fresno. The recipient of a Massachusetts Artists Foundation Fellowship Award and a nominee for two Pushcart Prizes, Butts was a faculty member of Goddard College in Plainfield, Vermont, where he taught in the Bachelor of Fine Arts program in creative writing. He previously served as associate professor of English at Hesser College in Manchester, N.H., and had taught in poetry workshops at the University of New Hampshire and for the New Hampshire Writers' Project. In addition to his teaching, he had been involved in a number of literary projects and was co-editor, with his wife, poet S Stephanie, of the journal, *Crying Sky: Poetry & Conversation*.

About the '60s: The poems included here are from W.E. Butts' collection *Radio Times*. They are about his life at that age of change and searching during a decade that was politically and socially steeped in both.

Ana Castillo was born and raised in Chicago. She is a prolific and celebrated poet, novelist, short story writer, essayist, editor, playwright, translator and independent scholar. Among her award-winning, best-selling titles: novels include *So Far From God, The Guardians* and *Peel My Love like an Onion*. Her novel *Sapogonia* was a *New York Times* Notable Book of the Year. She received an American Book Award from the Before Columbus Foundation for her first novel, *The Mixquiahuala Letters*. Her other awards include a Carl Sandburg Award, a Mountains and Plains Booksellers Award, and fellowships from the NEA in fiction and poetry. Castillo is editor of *La Tolteca,* an arts and literary 'zine dedicated to the advancement of a world without borders and censorship. Castillo's collection of essays, *Massacre of the Dreamers: Essays on Xicanisma*, is considered one of the core documents of Latina scholarship. She holds an M.A from the University of Chicago and a Ph.D., University of Bremen, Germany, in American Studies and an honorary doctorate from Colby College.

About the '60s: I grew up in Chicago, a Chicana in a mostly black neighborhood. It was not a good time to be anything but black in my neighborhood. I was taunted, beaten, bullied and harassed daily. In the '60s I was but a fleck of lint in the navel of a waking giant, a small-boned girl growing up in a flat smack dab in the middle of a city that made national headlines on the six o' clock news every evening. My parents worked in factories, and only occasionally would my mother mention the protesters. But as a senior, I started a kind of underground paper about the eminent Revolution. I did almost all the writing and illustration. (I think I drew the red winged woman straddling a conga on Santana's *Abraxus* album cover.) I also did the publishing (i.e. photocopying at my job on the sneak) and distribution (the school).

Lorna Dee Cervantes has been a Professor of English at CUU Boulder for 19 years and a recent UC Regents Lecturer at UC

Berkeley. She is the author of five award-winning books of poetry including *Emplumada* (1981), and her last three from Wings Press, *Suenño* (2013), *Ciento: 100 100-Word Love Poems* (2011), and the five volume *Drive: The First Quartet* (2006). Recipient of a Lila Wallace *Reader's Digest* Award, two NEA Fellowships, two Pushcart Prizes, and numerous other awards, she makes a new home in Olympia, WA, writing fiction, poetry, nonfiction, screenplays, and reviving her ground-breaking press, Mango Publications.

About the '60s: A "teeny-bopper" deadhead in the '60s ("No, man. I ain't no hippie. I'm an Indian!"), I'm a girl who has yet to outgrow the '60s. A poet, then as now, I'm now a trained philosopher of axiology, the study of value/s, writing about the value of the values of that time, ancient virtues, and also writing a novel of the time where music is the protagonist set in San Francisco where I was born. Born on Hiroshima Day, I am a child of war and a lifetime lover of peace. Overwhelming and disproportionate losses in the Vietnam War witnessed by Chicanas/Indigenous Americans shape and inform this poem which quotes the music of "Cream," "I'm so glad..." (a revolutionary act).

Kevin Clark's book *Self-Portrait with Expletives* won the Lena-Miles Wever Todd Poetry Book Competition and was published by Pleiades Press (2010). His first collection *In the Evening of No Warning* (New Issues Press, 2002) earned a grant from the Academy of American Poets. Kevin has published poems in the *Georgia, Iowa,* and *Antioch* reviews, *Crazyhorse, Ploughshares, Gulf Coast,* and *The Denver Quarterly.* One of his poems is anthologized in *The Notre Dame Review: The First Ten Years.* He has also won the Angoff Award from *The Literary Review.* A regular critic for *The Georgia Review,* Kevin has also published essays in *The Iowa Review, The Southern Review,* and *Contemporary Literary Criticism.* Pearson Longman publishes Kevin's poetry writing textbook *The Mind's Eye.* He teaches at Cal Poly and The Rainier Writing Workshop, and he lives with his wife Amy Hewes on California's central coast, where he plays city softball "despite legs like ancient concrete and more injuries than Evel Knievel." Kevin's web site with bio and email link is: http://kevinclarkpoet.com.

About the '60s: Originally on a track scholarship, I was at the University of Florida from 1968 to 1973, where I added poetry to the sex, drugs, and rock 'n' roll countercultural cocktail. The poem included here is based on a true story. After graduation I moved for a brief time to my home in suburban New Jersey, the scene for much of "Eight Hours in the Nixon Era."

Ginny Lowe Connors is the author of two poetry collections: *The Unparalleled Beauty of a Crooked Line* (2012) and *Barbarians in the Kitchen* (2005) as well as a chapbook, *Under the Porch* (2010), winner of the Sunken Garden Poetry Prize. In addition, she has edited several anthologies. She's won numerous awards for her poetry, including the Atlanta Review International Poetry Competition, and various prizes sponsored by the National Federation of State Poetry Societies, including their top prize, The Founders Award. Several years ago she was named the NEATE (New England Association of Teachers of English) "Poet of the Year." Connors has an M.F.A. in poetry from Vermont College of Fine Arts. A member of the executive board of the Connecticut Poetry Society, she also runs a small poetry press, Grayson Books. Connors served as West Hartford, Connecticut's poet laureate from 2013-2015. www.ginnyloweconnors.com.

About the '60s: I attended high school in Connecticut in the late 60's and college in New Hampshire while some of the most strident anti-war demonstrations erupted. "Optical Longings and Illusions" encapsulates some of my high school experiences. While some of my peers were insisting, "America: Love it or leave it," I joined marches against our country's participation in the Vietnam War and knew many young men who served overseas. As I was sleeping beneath the Washington Monument during the night of a protest demonstration, my sneakers were stolen. This made hitchhiking back to New Hampshire difficult. "Reunion" is an attempt to capture the feeling of this time.

Jim Daniels' fourteenth book of poems, *Birth Marks*, was published by BOA Editions in 2013 and was selected as a Michigan Notable Book, winner of the Milton Kessler Poetry Book Award, and received the Gold Medal in Poetry in the

Independent Publishers Book Awards. His fifth book of short stories, *Eight Mile High,* published by Michigan State University Press in 2014, was also selected as a Michigan Notable Book. His poems have been featured on Garrison Keillor's "Writer's Almanac," in Billy Collins' *Poetry 180* anthologies, and Ted Kooser's "American Life in Poetry" series. His poem "Factory Love" is displayed on the roof of a race car. His poems have appeared in the Pushcart Prize and *Best American Poetry* anthologies. A native of Detroit, Daniels is the Thomas Stockham University Professor of English at Carnegie Mellon University.

About the '60s: I spent part of the '60s in the basement of my parents' house getting stoned and listening to albums with my friends—the inspiration for a couple of these poems—and part living in a communal household with other hippie writers and artists, which inspired the other poem. "Wild Thing," as performed by Jimi Hendrix, is still my national anthem.

Kate Daniels is the author of four books of poetry, the most recent of which is *A Walk in Victoria's Secret.* Her poems appear in more than sixty anthologies, and she has received a Guggenheim Fellowship, a Pushcart Prize, and the Bunting Fellowship, among other honors. She is director of creative writing at Vanderbilt University, and lives in Nashville, Tennessee. A member of the Fellowship of Southern Writers, she was born and raised in Richmond, Virginia.

About the '60s: I was a kid and teenager, being raised up in Southside Richmond, Virginia—an area sometimes called Dogtown. My family was poor, white, working class, minimally educated—which is also sad to say, right wing and racist. Most of my family, including my dad, never finished high school. The men worked in factories, the women were clerks and secretaries. It was a marginalized, somewhat xenophobic world in all kinds of ways—poverty sliced us away from whites of means, race separated us from African Americans. I lived in an almost exclusively white world until I went to college, and had little feel for the politics and social change of the era. I missed much of the fervor of the '60s—then made up for lost time when I went to University of Virginia in 1971 as a scholarship kid.

Lucille Lang Day has published ten poetry collections and chapbooks, including *The Curvature of Blue*, *Infinities*, *Wild One*, and *The Book of Answers*. Her first poetry collection, *Self-Portrait with Hand Microscope*, received the Joseph Henry Jackson Award. She is also the author of a children's book, *Chain Letter*, and a memoir, *Married at Fourteen*, which received a 2013 PEN Oakland Josephine Miles Literary Award and was a finalist for the 2013 Northern California Book Award in Creative Nonfiction. Her poems, stories, and essays have appeared widely in magazines and anthologies, such as *The Cincinnati Review*, *The Hudson Review*, *Paterson Literary Review*, *Passages North*, *The Threepenny Review*, and *Times They Were A-Changing: Women Remember the '60s and '70s*. The founder and director of a small press, Scarlet Tanager Books, she earned her MA in English and MFA in creative writing at San Francisco State University, and her MA in zoology and PhD in science/mathematics education at the University of California, Berkeley. For more information, see http://lucil-lelangday.com. Twitter: @LucilleLDay.

About the '60s: I grew up in Piedmont, California, a town of about 11,000 completely surrounded by the much larger and more diverse city of Oakland. In 1960, when I turned thirteen, I was already cutting school, drinking, and shoplifting. I was also searching for "true love"which led to marrying at fourteen, giving birth at fifteen, divorcing at sixteen, and marrying the same man again at seventeen. I left him for the final time at eighteen because he didn't want me to go back to school. My poems came from a desire to explore this period of my life.

Toi Derricotte's most recent book is *The Undertaker's Daughter* (2011). Her honors include the 2012 Paterson Poetry Prize for Sustained Literary Achievement and the 2012 PEN/Voelcker Award for Poetry. Her poems have appeared in *The New Yorker*, *American Poetry Review*, and the *Paris Review*. With Cornelius Eady, she co-founded Cave Canem in 1996, and she is also a Chancellor of the Academy of American Poets.

About the '60s: In 1960, I was a freshman at Marygrove College, an all girls college in Detroit, Michigan, where I had been accepted to become an Immaculate Heart of Mary nun. The next year, I left Marygrove and became a student at Montieth College, an experimental college at Wayne State University, where the teachers were active professionals in their fields, rather than scholars. The following year, I was the mother of a child, living in the projects of Detroit, supporting myself by teaching at a job skills training center. In 1967, I married and moved to New York, where I took my first poetry workshop class, at The New School, and began my life as a poet.

Sally Lipton Derringer's book manuscript was a finalist for Fordham University's Poets Out Loud Prize and the New Issues Poetry Prize. She received honorable mention in *Nimrod's* Pablo Neruda Prize, was a runner-up for the Grolier Poetry Prize, a finalist for the *Glimmer Train* Poetry Open, an honorable mention in the poetry competition of the National Writers Union, a finalist for the Phyllis Smart Young Prize in Poetry, and a semifinalist for the Paumanok Poetry Award. Her poems have appeared in *Poet Lore, The Los Angeles Review, Sentence, Bellevue Literary Review, The Prose-Poem Project, Memoir, SLAB, The Quarterly, The New York Quarterly, Tampa Review,* and other journals and anthologies. She has an M.A. in Creative Writing from Antioch University, has taught in the English Department at SUNY Rockland, and currently teaches at Rockland Center for the Arts in West Nyack, N.Y.

 About the '60s: Home from my first year of college in the summer of 1971 and counting the days until I'd be going back for fall semester, I received a letter from the registrar's office informing me that the leave of absence I had requested had been granted. I had requested no leave, but as I stood next to the mailbox reading those words, I knew that my father had, in order to put a stop to the interracial relationship I was involved in. The '60s were over.

Rita Dove, U.S. Poet Laureate from 1993 to 1995, is the author of nine collections of poetry, including *Thomas and Beulah*, winner of the 1987 Pulitzer Prize, and most recently, *Sonata Mulattica*, a poetic treatise on the life of 19th-century violinist George Polgreen Bridgetower. Other book publications include short stories, essays, the novel *Through the Ivory Gate*, the drama *The Darker Face of the Earth* and, as its sole editor,

The Penguin Anthology of 20ᵗʰ-Century American Poetry. Ms. Dove received the 2011 National Medal of Arts from President Barack Obama and the 1996 National Humanities Medal from President Bill Clinton, making her the only poet with both presidential medals to her credit. Among her numerous other honors are the Heinz Award, the Duke Ellington Lifetime Achievement Award, the Emily Couric Leadership Award, the Common Wealth Award of Distinguished Service, and the Fulbright Lifetime Achievement Medal, as well as 25 honorary doctorates. Rita Dove is Commonwealth Professor of English at the University of Virginia.

About the '60s: On my eleventh birthday, I stood in front of a black and white TV in Washington D.C., trying to block out the raucous commentary of a horde of cousins I had never met before as I searched for my father among the blurry images of the crowd amassed in front of the Lincoln Memorial. August 28, 1963: I remember feeling pride, fear, and a *soupçon* of resentment, for this "March on Washington" had superceded my special day and infused it with anxiety. Later that evening, Dad back safe and sound, the celebration seemed to thread a direct line through me to a world beyond my horizon.

I was in high school during the late '60s, so most of my experiences with the explosive events in the wider world were peripheral. In the spring of 1970, however, I was chosen to be a Presidential Scholar, one of a select group of graduating seniors (two per state, plus fifteen at-large) invited to the White House to meet the president. By then the disastrous Cambodian Incursion was underway; two weeks before I received the Western Union telegram signed "Richard Nixon," at Kent State University—less than fifteen miles from my house in Akron, Ohio—four students had been shot dead by National Guardsmen. When we, the Presidential Scholars, convened in Washington on June 4, our collective plan to deliver an anti-war petition directly into Nixon's hands was prematurely uncovered (were we betrayed or bugged?); we received a scathing rebuke by H.R. Haldeman ("You should be grateful!"), and the medal-bestowing ceremony was downscaled to a presidential speech from a safe distance, with the boxed medals distributed by assistants as we exited the State Dining Room.

No matter: Ever since that brief moment when provincial

teenage idealism thudded against brutish central command power, I've never lost the acute sense of connection between the personal and the world, as well as a sense of our duty—as citizens and artists—to remain vigilant to the impact of roughshod external forces on the quotidian.

Stephen Dunn is the author of 17 collections of poetry, most recently *Lines of Defense* (Norton, 2013). His *Different Hours* was awarded the Pulitzer Prize.

    About the '60s: There was no particular occasion that spurred these two poems. Both are poems of memory. "The Sexual Revolution" was based on the actual so-called sexual revolution, which arrived about 3 or 4 years late to southern Minnesota, where I was living at the time. "Around the Time of the Moon" I wrote at Yaddo 30 years after the moon landing.

Jim Elledge's most recent books are a collection of poetry, *Tapping My Arm for a Vein*, and the biography *Henry Darger, Throwaway Boy: The Tragic Life of an Outsider Artist*. He's been awarded two Lambda Literary Awards, the first for his book-length poem *A History of My Tattoo* (2006) and the second for *Who's Yer Daddy? Gay Writers Celebrate Their Mentors and Forerunners* (2014), which he co-edited with David Groff. He directs the M.A. in Professional Writing Program at Kennesaw State University and lives in Atlanta.

    About the '60s: Like many of my contemporaries, I attended a university, marched against the war in Vietnam, did drugs, had sex—as much as possible—and read tons of poetry to try to figure it out. I'm still trying.

Martín Espada has published more than fifteen books as a poet, editor, essayist and translator. His forthcoming collection of poems is called *Vivas to Those Who Have Failed* (2016). Other books of poems include *The Trouble Ball* (2011), *The Republic of Poetry* (2006), and *Alabanza* (2003). His honors include the Shelley Memorial Award, the PEN/Revson Fellowship and a Guggenheim Fellowship. *The Republic of Poetry* was a finalist for the Pulitzer Prize. The title poem of his collection *Alabanza*, about 9/11, has been widely anthologized and performed. His book of essays, *Zapata's Disciple* (1998), was banned in Tucson as part of the Mexican-American Studies Program outlawed by the state of Arizona. A former tenant lawyer, Espada is a professor of English at the University of Massachusetts-Amherst.

About the '60s: All three poems take place in the East New York section of Brooklyn, where I was born in 1957, and all concern an evolution in consciousness characteristic of the 1960s. "Public School 190, Brooklyn 1963" recalls the Kennedy assassination in the context of the dim awareness that "something bad" was happening to us every day. "The Sign in My Father's Hands" chronicles my political awakening after my father's arrest for taking part in the CORE (Congress of Racial Equality) demonstrations at the New York World's Fair in 1964. "The Year I Was Diagnosed With a Sacrilegious Heart" deals with my own impromptu protest in 1969, triggered by the war in Vietnam and racism at home.

Sybil Pittman Estess just published her seventh book: *Like That: New and Selected Poems*, by Alamo Bay Press. It is available on Amazon. Estess has five books of poems, a co-edited book of criticism on Elizabeth Bishop, and a co-written textbook with Janet McCann, *In A Field of Words*. She has lived in Houston for thirty-seven years, but traveled widely and lived briefly in other places in the U.S. and abroad, such as England and Sicily. Sybil holds a B.A. from Baylor University, an M.A. from University of Kentucky, and a Ph.D. from Syracuse University. She has taught at various colleges in upstate New York, Kentucky, and Texas, and has published over one hundred and twenty essays, reviews, and poems, in a wide array of Texas and U.S. publications.

About the '60s: I was a student at Baylor University, traveling to and from my home in Mississippi, and in 1964-65, I taught school in my hometown, where the Klu Klux Klan was rampant. "In My Alice Blue Gown" is set in 1959, and is based on the lynching of Mack Charles Parker. Also during the 1960s, I married, lived in Kentucky and upstate New York in Syracuse, taught school, got a Master's degree. I was not active in but well aware of the Civil Rights Movement and the Anti-Vietnam protests. When I moved to upstate New York in the early 1970s, I became more engaged in alternative activities.

Susan Firer's most recent book is *Milwaukee Does Strange Things to People: New & Selected Poems 1979-2007*. Her previous books have been awarded the Cleveland State University Poetry Center Prize, the Posner Award, and the Backwaters Prize. She is a recipient of a Milwaukee County Artist Fellowship, a Wisconsin Arts Board Fellowship, the Lorine Niedecker Award, and in 2009 was given the University of Wisconsin-Milwaukee Distinguished Alumnus Award. Her poem "Call Me Pier" was included in the Poetry Foundation's Poetry Everywhere series and is available for viewing on YouTube and the Poetry Foundation's Poetry Everywhere website. Her poems "The Beautiful Pain of Too Much" and "Call Me Pier" have been choreographed by Janet Lilly and performed at St. Mark's in the Bowery, New York City, and at the 2010 Milwaukee Lakefront Festival of the Arts. From 2008-2010, she was Poet Laureate of the City of Milwaukee.

About the '60s: In 1966 I attended The University of Wisconsin-Oshkosh. After freshman year, convinced college was ruining my poetry, I hitchhiked to California, where I lived in a boarding house on the ocean, read Rilke, met Jim Morrison and filled notebooks with poems. I also attended love-ins at Griffith Park. In 1969, I revisited college, this time at The University of Wisconsin-Milwaukee. The summer after the campus strikes, I moved to Anchorage, AK. The '60s were a restless time for many. "Saint Valentine's Day, 1967" is an autobiographical poem that begins with my first Valentine's Day away from home.

Dede Fox attended Universidad de las Americas in Mexico D.F. and graduated from Washington University in St. Louis. TCU Press published her YA novel *The Treasure in the Tiny Blue Tin*, twice honored by the Association of Jewish Libraries. Her poetry has appeared in numerous anthologies, including *diverse-city*, *The Enigmatist*, *Poetica*, *Sol*, *A Summer's Poems*, *Swirl*, and *Texas Poetry Calendar*. "Chapultepec Park" won the 2008 Christina Sergeyevna Award at the Austin International Poetry Festival, and she has twice been a juried poet at Houston Poetry Fest. Her poetry books include *Confessions of a Jewish Texan*, Poetica Press, May 2013; and *Postcards Home*, Ink Brush

Press, 2014. An educator, Dede taught with Houston's Writer in the Schools and serves on the board of the Montgomery County Literary Arts Council.

About the '60s: In 1960, I was nine, reading *The Secret Garden* in sleepy Bellaire, Texas. During my 1961 *Jane Eyre* summer, my family drove to Toronto. Our return in February 1962 took us through Washington, D.C., where we witnessed Lyndon Johnson and John Glenn on the capitol steps. By 1965, I was a switchboard operator at a Jewish country club, other clubs banning Jews. A summer Head Start aide in 1967, I unknowingly integrated a Houston school. Before the 1968 pre-Olympic Tlatelolco massacre, I fled through Mexican troops armed with US weapons. The decade ended with my interviewing Howard Nemerov at Washington University.

Alice Friman's sixth full-length collection of poetry is *The View from Saturn*, LSU. Her previous book is *Vinculum* for which she won the 2012 Georgia Author of the Year Award in Poetry. She is a recipient of a 2012 Pushcart Prize and is included in *Best American Poetry 2009*. Other books include *The Book of the Rotten Daughter* and *Zoo*, which won the Sheila Margaret Motton Prize from The New England Poetry Club and the Ezra Pound Poetry Award from Truman State University. Her work appears in *The Georgia Review, Shenandoah, Boulevard, The Southern Review*, and many others. Friman is professor emerita of English and creative writing at the University of Indianapolis. Now she lives in Milledgeville, Georgia, where she is Poet-in-Residence at Georgia College. Her podcast series *Ask Alice* is sponsored by the Georgia College M.F.A. program and can be seen on YouTube.

About the '60s: In the '60s I was wheeling a baby carriage flanked by one kid on a tricycle and another on a bike with training wheels. To me the '60s were the '50s-plus until 1964 when I decided I had to change my life. I went back to school, studied literature, and began to write poems which I hid in a drawer for fourteen years until the women's movement came to Indiana and woke me up. "Dallas" and "Geometry" were written twenty years later in retrospect. "The Poet" is, sorry to say, how things were. Looking back, I'd say Gloria Steinem and poetry saved me.

Tess Gallagher's nine volumes of poetry include *Midnight Lantern: New and Selected Poems (2011); Dear Ghosts (2006); Moon Crossing Bridge (1992);* and *Amplitude (1997)*. Among her many other books are her translations of Liliana Ursu, *A Path to the Sea* (2011); *Barnacle Soup—Stories from the West of Ireland,* in collaboration with the Sligo storyteller Josie Gray (2008); and *Distant Rain,* a conversation with Jacucho Setouchi, of Kyoto. Gallagher is also the author of *Soul Barnacles: Ten More Years with Ray; A Concert of Tenses: Essays on Poetry,* and three collections of short fiction: *At the Owl Woman Saloon, The Lover of Horses and Other Stories,* and *The Man from Kinvara: Selected Stories* (2009). She wrote the preface for *Beyond Forgetting,* an anthology of poems about Alzheimer's. She also spearheaded the publication of Raymond Carver's *Beginners* in Library of America's collection of his stories (2009). She spends time in the West of Ireland and also lives and writes in Port Angeles, Washington.

About the '60s: In the 1980s, I was teaching at Squaw Valley, and I'd given my students an assignment: *write about something you've been putting off writing about.* I decided to write with them. The result was Sugarcane." It had been 18 years since the Vietnam War and the events described in the poem. I'd assumed that other wives of those who'd fought in the war might have experienced what I called the *psycho-erotic effects of the war.* No one had written about this—this strange surreal event of our government having flown the wives of fighter pilots to Hawaii to meet their warrior husbands in the middle of their 13-month tours. I was one of those wives. My poem bears witness.

Sandra M. Gilbert has published eight collections of poetry, most recently *Aftermath* (2011) and among prose books *Wrongful Death, Death's Door, Rereading Women,* and in 2014, *The Culinary Imagination: From Myth to Modernity* and *Eating Words: A Norton Anthology of Food Writing,* coedited with Roger Porter. Gilbert is currently at work on a new collection of poems, "Saturn's Meal," and with Susan Gubar, she is coauthor of *The Madwoman in the Attic* and other works: the two received the 2012 Award for Lifetime Achievement from the National Book Critics Circle.

About the '60s: In the '60s, I was raising three children, wearing paisley tunics, and moving from New York City to northern California, where I finished a dissertation on D. H. Lawrence, taught at two California State University campuses, and several of my kids, alas, drank Koolaid at People's Park—but fortunately their drinks were (I think) quite sobering.

H. Palmer Hall's most recent books are *Into the Thicket* (2011) and *Foreign and Domestic* (2009). His work has appeared in more than a hundred literary journals, including *North American Review, Ascent, The Connecticut Review, Texas Review, The Florida Review*, and many others. His poems and essays have been anthologized in *In a Fine Frenzy, American Diaspora, Letters to J. D. Salinger, In a Field of Words, Best Texas Writing, The Practice of Peace*, and other anthologies. Until he passed away in 2013, he was a librarian and teacher at St. Mary's University where he also served as editor of Pecan Grove Press.

About the '60s: Palmer spent the '60s in college and in Viet Nam. He went to his hometown university, Lamar, in Beaumont, Texas, but spent the last three years of the decade in the U. S. Army. First, he attended language school, learned Vietnamese and spent a year in that country as a linguist. Perhaps being a linguist kept the war personal for him; he translated intercepted radio messages, often listening to the same voice for many days while also knowing that others could be triangulating the speaker's location to call in a bomber. For many weeks he listened to a young guy coordinating Viet Cong patrols deep in the jungle. He translated the military messages of an enemy but also chuckled at the fellow's jokes and recognized the complaints soldiers everywhere make. When the voice abruptly stopped, he visualized the explosion blooming over the jungle. 1969 found Palmer in Washington at the National Security Agency where he continued to work as a translator. By then, his ambivalence about the war had hardened into opposition, and he signed the petition of active-duty soldiers against the war. When the Army attempted to strip him of his security clearance, he and others were successfully defended by the American Civil Liberties Union. As the '60s ended, the former Spec. 5 headed back to Texas and graduate school.

Barbara Hamby is the author of five books of poems, most recently *On the Street of Divine Love: New and Selected Poems* (2014) published by the University of Pittsburgh Press, which also published *Babel* (2004) and *All-Night Lingo Tango* (2009). She was a 2010 Guggenheim fellow in Poetry and her book of short stories, *Lester Higata's 20ᵗʰ Century*, won the 2010 Iowa Short Fiction Award. She teaches at Florida State University where she is Distinguished University Scholar.

About the '60s: During the '60s I lived in Honolulu and one of my passions was going to rock concerts. My first was the Rolling Stones in 1966. They were wearing faux Edwardian suits, and Brian Jones was still alive. But I was there for the Animals, who opened for the Stones. On the way back to England Chas Chandler, the Animals' bassist, discovered Jimi Hendrix in New York. I got to see Hendrix twice as well as Cream, and lots of other groups. I saw Jimi playing "The Star-Spangled Banner" on his knees with his teeth. It was all financed by babysitting.

Hunt Hawkins is currently Professor and Chair of the English Department at the University of South Florida. He previously taught at Florida State University, the University of Minnesota, Texas Southern University, and Kurasini College in Tanzania. Winner of the Agnes Lynch Starrett Prize in 1992, he published a book of poems, *The Domestic Life*, with the University of Pittsburgh Press in 1994. His poems have appeared in *Poetry*, *The Southern Review*, *The Georgia Review*, *Tri-Quarterly*, *The Minnesota Review*, and many other journals. He earned his Ph.D. at Stanford in 1976 and lived in many San Francisco Bay Area locations in the late 1960's and early 1970's.

About the '60s: Following college graduation in 1965, I spent a confused half-decade involving two graduate schools, teaching in Tanzania and Texas, and mainly avoiding the draft. It culminated, after turning draft-ineligible, in a year of not doing much. In winter 1969 I lived in Oakland in a "commune" of four people and constant crashers. All details of the poem are accurate, conveyed in a flat, reportorial style. It was written in 1977 after marriage and a steady job. I think my feeling then was dismay, maybe even disdain. Now decades later, I mainly feel nostalgia for the youthful energy of that time.

Edward Hirsch, a MacArthur Fellow, was born in Chicago, Illinois, in 1950. He has published nine books of poems, most recently *Gabriel: A Poem* (2014), a book-length elegy, and *The Living Fire: New and Selected Poems* (2010), which brings together thirty-five years of work. He has also published five prose books, among them *A Poet's Glossary* (2014), a complete compendium of poetic terms, and *How to Read a Poem and Fall in Love with Poetry* (1999), a national bestseller. He lives in New York and serves as president of the John Simon Guggenheim Memorial Foundation.

About the '60s: 1968 was the fault-line, the year I graduated from Niles West High School in Skokie, Illinois, a suburb of Chicago, and started Grinnell College, in Iowa, where I played Division III football and set out to become a poet. I was in the heart of the country, but the social revolution was in full swing. My high school girlfriend, for example, who later transferred to Grinnell, liked to trip on acid and sit with my parents at home games. I wrote these poems many years later, when everything had changed, and my own past—how it was interwoven into the times—suddenly seemed mysterious to me.

David Huddle is from Ivanhoe, Virginia, and he's lived in Vermont for 44 years. He's taught at the University of Vermont, Hollins University, Middlebury College, Goddard College, Johnson State College, Radford University, Austin Peay State University, The University of Idaho, The Bread Loaf School of English, The Rainier Writing Workshop, and The Sewanee School of Letters. His fiction, poetry, and essays have appeared in *The American Scholar, Esquire, Appalachian Heritage, The New Yorker, Harper's, Poetry, Story, Shenandoah, Agni, Green Mountains Review, The Sow's Ear, Plume,* and *The Georgia Review*. In 2012 his novel *Nothing Can Make Me Do This* won the Library of Virginia Award for Fiction, and his collection *Black Snake at the Family Reunion* won the Pen New England Award for Poetry. His recent novel is *The Faulkes Chronicle*, his new poetry collection is *Dream Sender*, and a new novel, *The Immaculate Assassin*, is scheduled for publication by Tupelo Press in 2016.

About the '60s: In 1966 I was sent to the 25th Military Intelligence Detachment, supporting the 25th Infantry Division in Cu Chi, Vietnam. I was discharged in the summer of 1967 from the Army and returned to the University of Virginia for summer school. "Work," "Nerves," and "Them" were written in the summer and fall of 1975, after I'd watched television coverage of the Fall of Saigon. The startling images I saw on TV made me realize that I was rapidly forgetting many details of my service in Vietnam, and I thought I should try to write as much as I could remember of that time. The poems came to be fourteen-liners, in part because I'd already begun writing sonnet sequences, and the form turned out to be very hospitable to what I could remember of my time in Vietnam.

Tim Hunt's publications include *Fault Lines* (2009, The Backwaters Press) and *The Tao of Twang* (2014, CW Books); and poems in such journals as *CutBank*, *Epoch*, *Quarterly West*, and *Rhino*. Twice nominated for the Pushcart Prize, he has been awarded the Chester H. Jones National Poetry Prize for "Lake County Elegy." His third collection, *Poem's Poems & Other Poems*, will be published in 2016 by CW Books. His scholarly publications include *The Textuality of Soulwork: Jack Kerouac's Search for Spontaneous Prose*, *Kerouac's Crooked Road: Development of a Fiction* and the five-volume edition *The Collected Poetry of Robinson Jeffers*. He is currently University Professor of English at Illinois State University. Originally from the quicksilver mining region of Northern California, he now lives with his wife, Susan, in Normal, where he is University Professor of English at Illinois State University.

      About the '60s: In 1966 I was a highschooler making weekend pilgrimages to the Fillmore, worrying about college admissions, and increasingly politicized by the draft and the Vietnam War. I was not a Woodstocker, in spite of my love of the music. The March on the Pentagon was, it seems, more the symbolic center of my '60s, and I believed, truly, in Eugene McCarthy. Peace doves, tie-dye, and the grieving dread of My Lai, Bobby Kennedy dead, Kent State, Detroit in flames. Ah, youth. Let's watch that movie again—but not the scene where Sly Stone takes us "Higher." Hendrix, the sea of garbage, "Purple Haze" and a "Star Spangled Banner."

David Jauss is the author of two poetry collections, *Improvising Rivers* and *You Are Not Here*; three short story collections,

Crimes of Passion, Black Maps, and *Glossolalia: New & Selected Stories*; and a collection of craft essays, *On Writing Fiction.* He has also edited or coedited three anthologies, including *Strong Measures: Contemporary American Poetry in Traditional Forms.* His poems have appeared in such journals as *The Georgia Review, The Missouri Review, The Nation, Paris Review, Ploughshares, Poetry,* and *Shenandoah* and been reprinted in numerous anthologies, including *The Poetry Anthology: Ninety Years of America's Most Distinguished Verse Magazine.* The recipient of a National Endowment for the Arts Fellowship, the Fleur-de-Lis Poetry Prize, the AWP Award for Short Fiction, a James A. Michener Fellowship, two Pushcart Prizes, and an O. Henry Prize, he teaches in the low-residency M.F.A. in Writing Program at Vermont College of Fine Arts.

About the '60s: I spent the 1960s in Montevideo, Minnesota, my hometown, playing baseball, dragging Main Street, lying in a hospital with a broken back that kept me out of Vietnam, wooing my future wife, and writing my first poems, all of which imitated a fellow Minnesotan from a town three hundred miles north on Highway 61. "Beauty" was inspired by Jackie Kennedy's account of her husband's assassination in a 1963 interview with Theodore White. "The Border" was an attempt to imagine my way into the mind and heart of a high school friend who returned from the war much changed.

David Kirby's collection *The House on Boulevard St.: New and Selected Poems* was a finalist for the National Book Award in 2007. Kirby is the author of *Little Richard: The Birth of Rock 'n' Roll,* which the *Times Literary Supplement* of London called "a hymn of praise to the emancipatory power of nonsense. His most recent poetry collection is *A Wilderness of Monkeys.* For more information, see www.davidkirby.com.

About the '60s: Then as now, I spent my time trying to reconcile a love of pleasure with the satisfaction I take in hard work. As an undergraduate, I lived on a farm under the gaze of my parents, so imagine my joy when I went off to graduate school in the great city of Baltimore in 1966. I spent my days there learning as much as I could and my nights seeking the trippiest drugs, the grooviest concerts, and the most pliant women. Try as hard as I did at those pursuits, I came to find out that I wasn't much of a rascal, even though I desperately wanted to be one. In that time, I got a lot of work done. And I did take some great drugs. And went to some groovy concerts.

Yusef Komunyakaa's books of poetry include *Taboo, Dien Cai Dau, Neon Vernacular* (for which he received the Pulitzer Prize), *The Chameleon Couch,* and most recently *The Emperor of Water Clocks* (FSG). He has been the recipient of numerous awards including the William Faulkner Prize (Université Rennes, France), the Kingsley Tufts Award for Poetry, the Ruth Lilly Poetry Prize, the Poetry Society of America's Shelley Memorial Award, and the 2011 Wallace Stevens Award. His plays, performance art and libretti have been performed internationally, and include *Slipknot, Wakonda's Dream, Nine Bridges Back, Saturnalia, Testimony, The Mercy Suite,* and *Gilgamesh* (a verse play) with Chad Gracia. He teaches at New York University.

About the '60s: I drew a slew of sketches of greenhouses and planted azaleas around my father's three acres. Also, James Baldwin's *Notes of a Native Son, Nobody Knows My Name,* and *The Fire Next Time*. I thought I'd become an essayist. Then, Sam Cooke cut "A Change Is Gonna Come," daring some to embrace more audacious dreams. One Sunday afternoon, my neighbor Lorraine (Nina Simone's look-alike) and I decided to sit in the all-white section of the State Theater on Columbia Street, where I had sat many times peering down from the balcony. When we approached the ticket booth to pay our fee, the woman behind the glass said, "I suppose you wanna sit down here." We nodded yes, entered, and sat close to the center aisle. Soon the seats filled around us. Lorraine placed her 25 cal. automatic into my hand and I froze. I tried to brace myself, but something snapped my head around and I saw policemen lined across the rear of the theater. The lights dimmed. I don't remember a single image from the *Lawrence of Arabia* rerun. And I don't know exactly why I took to Vietnam, in 1969, Donald Allen's *New American Poetry* and Ann Fairbairm's *Five Smooth Stones,* but I do know that was when poetry overtook me.

Ted Kooser served two terms as the U. S. Poet Laureate from 2004-2006, and during his second term he was awarded the Pulitzer Prize for his collection, *Delights & Shadows* (Copper Canyon Press). He serves as Presidential Professor English at the University of Nebraska-Lincoln. His most recent books are *Splitting an Order* (Copper Canyon Press) and *The Wheeling Year* (University of Nebraska Press). He lives in rural Nebraska.

About the '60s: My first wife and I were divorced in 1970 and I remained single for the next seven years. During those years, when everybody I knew seemed to be enjoying guiltless sex and shunning commitments, I was miserably lonely, wanting to find someone to love. I'd very much hoped the young woman in "Shame" might be the one, but I hadn't the courage.

Judy Kronenfeld's most recent books of poetry are *Shimmer* (Word Tech Editions, 2012), and the second edition of *Light Lowering in Diminished Sevenths* (Antrim House, 2012), winner of the 2007 Litchfield Review Poetry Book Prize. Her poems have appeared in many print and online journals such as *American Poetry Review, Calyx, Cimarron Review, Natural Bridge, The Pedestal, Sequestrum, Valparaiso Poetry Review,* and *The Women's Review of Books.* They have also appeared in eighteen anthologies, including *Before There Is Nowhere to Stand: Palestine/Israel: Poets Respond to the Struggle* (Lost Horse, 2012), and *Beyond Forgetting: Poetry and Prose about Alzheimer's Disease* (Kent State, 2009). Her more occasional stories and essays have appeared in *Literary Mama* and *Under the Sun,* among others. She is Lecturer Emerita, Creative Writing Department, UC Riverside, and an Associate Editor of the online poetry journal, *Poemeleon.* Visit her on the web at http://judykronenfeld.com.

About the '60s: I was a graduate student in English literature during the middle '60s, then out of the country, at a great remove, during much of the excitement of the later '60s (dissertation research in Ghana—my husband's—and England—mine). Came back to the U.S. and finished that dissertation in 1969-70. The young protagonist from whose embarrassment this poem grew has asked me not to blow her cover.

Maxine Kumin was the recipient of numerous awards, including the Eunice Tietjens Memorial Prize for Poetry (1972), the Pulitzer Prize for Poetry (1973) for *Up Country*, in 1995 the Aiken Taylor Award for Modern American Poetry, the 1994 Poets' Prize (for *Looking for Luck*), an American Academy and Institute of Arts and Letters award for excellence in literature (1980), an Academy of American Poets fellowship (1986), and the 1999 Ruth Lilly Poetry Prize. In 1981–1982, she served as the poetry consultant to the Library of Congress. She taught poetry in New England College's Low-Residency MFA Program. She was also a contributing editor at *The Alaska Quarterly Review*. Together with fellow-poet Carolyn Kizer, she first served on and then resigned from the board of chancellors of the Academy of American Poets, an act that galvanized the movement for opening this august body to broader representation by women and minorities. She died in 2014.

David Lehman, a native New Yorker, did his undergraduate work at Columbia University from 1966 to 1970. He is the editor of *The Oxford Book of American Poetry*, the series editor of *The Best American Poetry* (which he launched in 1988), and the author of *New and Selected Poems* (2009) among other collections. His nonfiction book *A Fine Romance: Jewish Songwriters, American Songs* won the 2010 Deems Taylor Award from ASCAP. He teaches in the graduate writing program at the New School and lives in New York City with his wife, Stacey.

    About the '60s: In 1966 I entered Columbia, idealistic, ambitious. The political event dominating everyone's consciousness during my college years was the war in Vietnam, which tore the nation apart. The 1960s had begun with infinite promise—youth, vitality, the hope attached to our new president, the re-birth of the cool (as epitomized by, say, Sinatra, Audrey Hepburn, Johnny Carson, and James Bond), the triumph of American painting (Abstract-Expressionism, Pop Art), some very good jazz, some outstanding experimental writing (poetry and prose). The period ended in despondency, but the tumult and turbulence along the way were terribly exciting to one in his late teens and early twenties living in New York City and attending Columbia University, where student demonstrations made front-page headlines in April 1968.

Adrian C. Louis is a half-breed Indian, born and raised in northern Nevada and is an enrolled member of the Lovelock Paiute Tribe. From 1984-97, Louis taught at Oglala Lakota College on the Pine Ridge Reservation of South Dakota. He recently retired as Professor of English at Minnesota State University in Marshall. He has written ten books of poems and two works of fiction. Louis has won various awards including two Pushcart Prizes and fellowships from the Bush Foundation, the National Endowment for the Arts, and the Lila Wallace-Reader's Digest Foundation. More info at www. Adrian-C-Louis.com.

About the '60s: For me, the '60s ran from '65 to '72. During those years I flunked out of college, sold weed, hitched across America several times, and lived in the Haight-Ashbury during its heyday. For my account of those years, my book of poems entitled *Ancient Acid Flashing Back* is available from the University of Nevada Press.

Janet Lowery's poetry has appeared in literary reviews such as *Poetry East, Greensboro Review, California Quarterly, Concho River Review, Pennsylvania English,* and *Christianity and Literature*; in anthologies such as *Women's Blood* (Continuing SAGA Press, 1981), the *Poetry East* anthology *Who Are the Rich and Where Do They Live?* (2000); *Texas in Poetry 2* (TCU Press, 2002); and *Improbable Worlds,* the 2011 anthology from Mutabilis Press. A chapbook, *Thin Dimes,* was published by Wings Press (1992). Her trilogy of plays, *Traffic in Women,* was produced 2006-2008 at the University of St. Thomas, Houston, where she teaches full-time in the English Department. Odonata House published monologues from the plays in 2008. Her latest play, *A Heroine-Free Summer,* will be produced by Mildred's Umbrella Theatre Company in Houston during the 2016-2017 season. She is a licensed massage therapist, practitioner of Reconnective Healing, and consultant for the holistic aspects of UST's Nursing Program.

About the '60s: In the late '60s I was in high school in upstate New York. Involved in gymnastics, and later, modern dance, I listened to rock music (like most of us) and discussed lyrics with my siblings and friends, some of us becoming increasingly involved in alcohol and drug abuse. I wrote poems about racial inequality and other issues, but worried about those I knew who became addicted to hard drugs in the aftermath of that magical period of social upheaval we call the '60s. Alcoholism/drug addiction is still one of the most stigmatized diseases in the world. In October 2014, I lost a nephew, Sam Lowery, to the modern-day scourge.

George Ella Lyon's most recent poetry collections are *Many-Storied House* (University Press of Kentucky, 2013) and *She Let Herself Go,* (LSU, 2012). Her other work includes a novel, a memoir, and a short story collection as well as thirty-seven books for young readers. She has received an Al Smith Fellowship, residencies at the Hambidge Center for the Arts, numerous grants from The Kentucky Foundation for Women, a Pushcart Prize nomination, and is featured in the PBS series, *The United States of Poetry.* A native of Harlan County, Kentucky, Lyon works as a freelance writer and teacher based in Lexington. She is co-author with J. Patrick Lewis of *Voices from the March on Washington* (2014), one of *Booklist's* Top Ten Multicultural Titles for YA's and winner of the Cybils Award for Poetry. She is Poet Laureate of Kentucky for 2015-2016. For more information visit www.georgeellalyon.com.

About the '60s: During the '60s, I grew from a fifth grader to a junior in college, from putting on plays in a Quonset-hut classroom to demonstrating for civil rights and against the Vietnam War at my small college in Kentucky.

Mary Travers sang her way into my heart with Peter Paul and Mary's first album (1962). An eighth grader, I hastened to Cumberland Valley Music Company and traded my flute and ten dollars for a guitar. Soon I was writing songs and performing with my best friend. Gone were my dreams of being a zookeeper. I planned to head for Greenwich Village the minute I graduated.

My parents thought this a bad idea, and I didn't have the nerve to go it alone. Instead, I went to Centre College with the understanding that after one year my parents would reconsider. As they'd hoped, I found friends there I didn't want to leave. But I kept Mary's voice and witness close. Over fifty years later, I still write and perform, most recently when I was inducted

as Kentucky's Poet Laureate. Playing the washboard in the
Capitol Rotunda, I sang "Creed" which begins:

> I am not the you of you
> And you are not the me of me
> But we're here in solidarity
> Brothers, sisters, One One One One
> Brothers, sisters: One.

Bonnie Lyons retired in May 2014 with emeritus status and a
UTSA President's Award for Creative Excellence after teach-
ing for 38 years at UTSA. She has published three chapbooks
(*Hineni, Meanwhile,* and *So Far*) and two full-length books
of poetry (*In Other Words* and *Bedrock*). Individual poems
have appeared in many journals. She has also published a
book about Henry Roth and *Call It Sleep* as well as *Passion
and Craft*, a book of literary interviews with fiction writers.
Miriam Talks Back, a CD of her reading some of her biblical
poem has recently been produced. Being Wendy Barker's col-
league and friend since Wendy joined the department is one
of Bonnie's great joys.

    About the '60s: My poem, "Mother to Daughter, 1960"
is about my mother and our embattled relationship when I
was 16, still living at home. Later in the '60s I went to and
graduated from college, worked in New York at Bantam
Books, married and moved to Stockton, CA, where I was a
Probation Officer at age 21 with only a B.A. in English, then
spent a year in Israel teaching Jewish children from Arab
countries. I returned to California where I worked as a social
worker while all my friends were hippies and produced under-
ground comics. That year in San Francisco (1968-1969) I was
in the heart of the '60s action. When I left to go to graduate
school in New Orleans, my friends, having just seen "Easy
Rider," warned me I'd be killed on the way.

Paul Mariani is the University Professor of English at Boston
College, specializing in Modern American and British Poetry,
religion and literature, and creative writing. He has published
over 200 essays, chapters in anthologies, and reviews, as well
as being the author of 18 books. These include biographies
of William Carlos Williams, John Berryman, Robert Lowell,

Hart Crane, Gerard Manley Hopkins, and Wallace Stevens. Mariani has published seven volumes of poetry. He is also the author of *Thirty Days: On Retreat with the Exercises of St. Ignatius*. His awards include a Guggenheim Fellowship and several National Endowment for the Arts and National Endowment for the Humanities Fellowships. His biography of Williams was a Finalist for the NBA. In 2009 he received the John Ciardi Award for Lifetime Achievement in Poetry. His life of Hart Crane, *The Broken Tower*, a feature-length film, directed by and starring James Franco, was released in 2012. He is now at work on a memoir of growing up on the mean streets of New York in the 1940s and an eighth volume of poetry, *Ordinary Time*.

About the '60s: In 1959, I met the woman I would marry in 1963, and by whom I would have three sons in the next five years. During that iconic decade, I finished up at Manhattan College, spent two years at Colgate pursuing my Master's and teaching freshmen comp, then four years living with my growing family in a tiny apartment in Flushing, taking the subway each day into Manhattan to pursue my doctorate at the City University of New York, where I was fortunate enough to have Allen Mandelbaum for a mentor, and where I eked out a living (barely) teaching at Hunter, Lehmann, and the John Jay College of Criminal Justice, Frank Serpico being one of the many cops I taught. In 1968, having completed my dissertation on Gerard Manley Hopkins, I began teaching English core courses at UMass/ Amherst, where I witnessed the student unrest which culminated in the nightmarish shutting down of the university following the Kent State killings. I vividly remember the deaths of the Kennedys, King and Malcolm X, the miasma of Viet Nam, the racial tensions, the Beatles, and so much more.

Beverly Matherne's sixth bilingual book, *Bayou des Acadiens / Blind River*, a collection of short stories and prose poems, is from Éditions Perce-Neige. She has done over 300 readings across the U.S., Canada, and France and in Wales, Belgium, Germany, and Spain. Special venues include Tulane University, Cornell University, Shakespeare and Company in Paris, and the United Nations in New York. She is one of eight authors, including Samuel Beckett and Vladimir Nabokov, whose bilingual writing process is the subject of a completed doctoral dissertation from the University of Paris III. Widely published, she has received seven first-place prizes, including the Hackney Literary Award for Poetry, and four Pushcart nominations. Professor Emerita of English at Northern Michigan University, she served as director of the MFA program in creative writing (four years), director of the Visiting Writers Series (seven years) and poetry editor of *Passages North* literary magazine (four years).

About the '60s: While an art student at University of Louisiana, at Lafayette, pictures of students killed in Vietnam were posted daily in the Student Union. Unbelievably, my brother Curtis, Jr., was drafted. Surprisingly, he came back intact and resumed his college studies. Picking me up for the holidays at the end of the semester, he lugged into the trunk of his car my huge op art piece, consisting of stripes and flashing lights powered by a lawn mower motor. On the way home, I wax sculpted his ear. The poem is a tribute to his last day, death, and burial.

Janet McCann explores faith and the passage of time. Her collections include *Looking for Buddha in the Barbed-Wire Garden* (1996), *Emily's Dress* (2004), and *Pascal Goes to the Races* (2004). McCann has coedited, with David Craig, the faith-based anthologies *Odd Angles of Heaven* (1994), *Place of Passage* (2000), and *Francis and Clare in Poetry* (2005). Her honors include a fellowship from the National Endowment for the Arts. She is a professor at Texas A&M University and lives in College Station, Texas.

About the '60s: In 1964 I was in grad school at Pitt, but I went to Chicago often to visit my fiancé (now husband) who was at the University of Chicago. The guys at seminary were friends who liked to attend our parties—but were not allowed to—so would sneak across the campus in their black priest duds to meet our car at the other side of the fence. As for the Coke Machine poem, silver dime just brought back those events. I had a wonderful '60s—student marriage in Chicago—protests and vigils—truly believed we all were fixing things.

Bryce Milligan was the founding editor of *Pax: A Journal for Peace Through Culture* and *Vortex: A Critical Review*. For several years he was the book critic for the *San Antonio Express-News* and the *San Antonio Light*. Later he directed the Guadalupe Cultural Arts Center's literature program and its San Antonio Inter-American Book Fair. He was the primary editor of two major collections of Latina writing: *Daughters of the Fifth Sun* (Riverhead, 1995) and *¡Floricanto Sí!* (Penguin, 1997). He has been the publisher, editor, and book designer of Wings Press since 1995. Milligan is the author of four historical novels and short story collections for young adults. One of his children's books, *Brigid's Cloak*, was a 2002 "Best of the Year" pick by *Publisher's Weekly* and Bank Street College. He has published seven collections of poetry, including *Alms for Oblivion* (London: Aark Arts, 2003) and the forthcoming *Take to the Highway: Arabesques for Travelers* (West End Press, 2016). His poetry and song lyrics have also appeared in numerous literary magazines. Recipient of Gemini Ink's Award for Literary Excellence (2011), he also received the President's Peace Commission's "Art of Peace Award" (2012) from St. Mary's University. His website is http://www. brycemilligan.com.

About the '60s: In the late '60s I was still in high school in Dallas, apprenticed to a luthier (Don Berry) and singing folk music at the Rubaiyat, where I was very lucky to be mentored by the likes of Townes Van Zandt, Steve Frumholz, and B.W. Stevenson. (Best—and most brutal—creative writing classes *ever*.) There was little activism in Dallas, but we tried, mainly by singing protest songs, wearing black arm bands and using the school's mimeograph machine at night to produce anti-war fliers. SDS was just a dream some of us had. The real revolution, as Joy Harjo has pointed out, was love.

Kent Newkirk is a self-taught poet, longtime former newspaper editor, now working blue-collar labor, mostly cooking at a cross-country ski center and local resort restaurant, choosing to pay for his writing time with jobs he can leave behind when he punches the clock, largely dropping out in order to tune in, living with his love in a camp on top of a notoriously harsh mountain in rural Vermont, hauling water, burning wood, devoting his writing life to poetry. He saw Hendrix, protested, tripped on acid, and jokes, "I was there on the front lines of the Sexual Revolution!" But now in his 60s looking back at the Sixties, he thinks future generations will point to the sea changes in the relationships between sexes as the high-water-mark movement of our lifetime. "Sex Education" and "Tripping Through Life, Fantastic" are paeans to love and times gone by. He's had work published in *Rattle, Blue Collar Review, Margie,* and is a past winner of the "Working People's Poetry Competition" from *Partisan Press.*

About the '60s: "Sex Education" and "Tripping Through Life, Fantastic" are paeans to love and times gone by, but it's the music that resonates to this day. Entering high school in 1969, I was the kid with his ears glued to headphones and Boston's *WBCN*, the cutting edge of rock. Public school held no interest; there was too much history going on right out the front door. Peace marches, girls, and music. It was impossible to trust authority, a lesson force-fed to us repeatedly. I became a reporter to confront my own ignorance by asking questions, a poet to find some answers. Still searching.

Carol A. Newman is a graduate of the English program at the University of Pittsburgh at Bradford. Her M.A. in English was completed at St. Bonaventure University. At Pitt-Bradford she teaches beginning and advanced poetry writing as well as classes in fiction and creative non-fiction writing. In 2012, she was the recipient of the Hauser Award in Prose in the Chautauqua Literary Arts contest as well as winning second place, and an honorable mention in poetry that year. Her essay "Pens" was published in the 2013 issue of *Chautauqua Magazine.* Her most recent publication is a poem entitled "Birth Rite" in the anthology *Written on Water: Writings About the Allegheny River* published by May Apple Press 2013.

About the '60s: In the early 1960s, I was in junior high school, just out of sixth grade, still starry eyed over the promise of the space program. None of us knew it then, but we were on the cusp of the sexual revolution and Vietnam. My poem grew from the reflection on that rapid transition from complete innocence to knowledge; what we *thought* was ahead of us, and what came to be. Nineteen fifty-nine, for me, represents that last joyous breath of total innocence.

Alicia Ostriker is a poet and critic whose first book of poems, *Songs*, appeared in 1969. Her thirteenth poetry collection, *The Book of Seventy*, received the 2009 National Jewish Book Award for Poetry; *The Book of Life: Selected Jewish Poems 1979-2011* received a Paterson Lifetime Achievement Award in 2013. She has also received awards from the Poetry Society of America, the San Francisco Poetry Center, the Guggenheim foundation and the Rockefeller Foundation among others, and has twice been a National Book Award finalist. Her most recent book of poems is *The Old Woman, the Tulip, and the Dog*. As a critic, Ostriker is the author of *Stealing the Language: the Emergence of Women's Poetry in America*, and has published several other books on poetry and on the Bible. She is Professor Emerita of Rutgers University and teaches in the Low-Residency MFA Program of Drew University.

About the '60s: For me, the '60s began in 1965. I'd voted for Johnson so he would end the Vietnam War. He didn't. Rutgers was a boys school then, and teaching was a joy since they all hated the war and wanted to alter and expand their minds. I wanted to do that too. And I liked to dance. The '60s ended for me in 1973, when I returned from a mind-expanding sabbatical in Berkeley and realized the dream was over for my students. It's never been over for me. My poems all speak to the dream, to try to keep it alive.

Dave Parsons, 2011 Texas Poet Laureate, grew up in Austin. He joined the U.S. Marine Corps Reserve in 1961. Parsons attended U.T. Austin and Texas State University, receiving a BBA. After short careers of owning a haberdashery and Ad Agency, he moved to Houston to teach Marketing and Coach baseball and basketball at Bellaire High. He received his MA from the University of Houston's Graduate Creative Writing Program in 1991. Parsons has taught Creative Writing and has coached the Handball/Racquetball Club/Team at Lone Star College since 1992 and lives in Conroe, Texas with his wife Nancy, an award winning fine artist & graphic designer. Parsons was a recipient of a N.E.H. Dante Fellowship to SUNY, the French-American Legation Poetry Prize, and the Baskerville Publisher's Prize. He was inducted into The Texas Institute of Letters in 2009. He has published six collections of poetry; his latest is *Reaching For Longer Water*. www.daveparsonspoetry.com.

About the '60s: In 1961, my senior year at Austin High, I joined the U.S. Marine Corps Reserve. I returned from six months training and worked as a welder's helper for a bridge company until school began. I spent the next six years bouncing between SWTSU (now Texas State University) and The University of Texas, where I walked out under the tower 40 minutes before Whitman began shooting, the same day as the 100th anniversary of Scholz Beer Garden. Seeing Lyndon Johnson around Austin was not unusual, since his ranch was an hour or so away. I lived a half mile from Barton Springs, a world-famous natural spring-fed pool. I worked summers there as a lifeguard. The swimming pool was also fed by Barton Creek, where the group of kids I grew up with would play. It was our own world away from the world. The poems came to me from these memories and experiences.

Robert Phillips is the author of over 30 books. His prizes include an award in Literature from The American Academy and Institute of Arts and Letters.

Stanley Plumly was called "the successor to James Wright and John Keats, with a marvelous ear for the music of contemplation" by Rita Dove. Plumly's most recent collection of poems is *Orphan Hours* (Norton, 2012). In 2014 he published *The Immortal Evening: A Legendary Dinner With Keats, Wordsworth, and Lamb* (Norton), which won the Truman Capote Prize for Literary Criticism. Earlier books include *Old Heart* (named the *Los Angleles Times Book Review*'s Poetry Book of the Year), *Now That My Father Lies Down Beside Me,* and *The Marriage in the Trees*. Other honors won by the Maryland State Poet Laureate include a Guggenheim Fellowship, three NEA Fellowships, the Ingram-Merrill Foundation Award, and six Pushcart Prizes.

About the '60s: My only comment on the '60s is that I hope the mix of promise, tragedy, and stupidity will not be repeated—but, then, here we are.

Andrea Potos' latest poetry collections are *New Girl* (Anchor & Plume Press), and *We Lit the Lamps Ourselves* (Salmon Poetry,

Ireland). Another book from Salmon is forthcoming in 2015. She is also the author of three other collections: *Yaya's Cloth* (Iris Press); *Abundance to Share With the Birds* (Finishing Line Press), and *The Perfect Day* (Parallel Press). Her work appears widely in print and online. She has received the James Hearst Poetry Prize from the *North American Review,* and two Outstanding Achievement Awards in Poetry from the Wisconsin Library Association. She lives in Madison, Wisconsin with her husband and daughter.

About the '60s: In the '60s, I was growing up in Milwaukee, Wisconsin and attending Henry Clay Elementary School. I had a huge gaggle of girlfriends, and it seemed we were constantly immersed in having parties and sleepovers. My father worked for the local TV station, and so TV held an important place in our house. Shows I loved included, of course, sexy Tom Jones (I was also boy-crazy), *Lost in Space, Gilligan's Island, Dark Shadows*, and, on autumn Sundays the ever-fabulous Green Bay Packers.

Alberto Ríos, Arizona's inaugural poet laureate and a chancellor of the Academy of American Poets, was born in Nogales, Arizona, and he has written from that geographic and sociological perspective through five decades. His eleven collections of poetry include, most recently, *A Small Story about the Sky*, and *The Smallest Muscle in the Human Body*, a finalist for the National Book Award. He has also written three short story collections and a memoir about growing up on the Mexican border, *Capirotada*. Ríos is the host of the PBS program Books & Co., and has taught at Arizona State University since 1982.

About the '60s: In the '60s, I was still in high school, living on the Arizona border with Mexico, looking for a language and a place of my own. I was a first generation American—my father came from Mexico and my mother from England, but everything got mixed up in this place I was living—wonderfully so. While the world was asking me to choose my life, I was learning that it wasn't *either-or* but *also-and*. The '60s gave me open arms and the sensibility to understand that everything— Spanish, English, Border, Yaqui, slang, all of it—was my language and my thinking. The border was a perfect metaphorical geography for all this—it was the edge and the middle both for me. I was writing, I was singing, I was talking, I was acting, I was painting, but most of all I was thinking: inside of me was a loud place.

Danny Romero was born and raised in Los Angeles. He has a BA from UC Berkeley and an MA from Temple University in Philadelphia. He is the author of the novel *Calle 10* (Mercury House) and a book of poetry *Traces* (Bilingual Review Press). He lives in Sacramento, CA and teaches at Sacramento City College.

About the '60s: I was born in 1961. I am the youngest of seven children with 4 older brothers and two older sisters. I learned a lot about the world from them all.

Paul Ruffin, 2009 Texas State Poet Laureate, is a Texas State University System Regents' Professor, and Distinguished Professor of English at Sam Houston State University. He is founder and Editor of the *Texas Review* and Director of Texas Review Press. His award winning stories and poems have appeared in many of the most prestigious journals and magazines. He also writes a newspaper column, *Ruffin It*. Ruffin's books include two novels, six collections of short stories, four books of essays, and seven collections of poetry. He has also edited/co-edited fifteen other books.

About the '60s: When I was growing up in poverty on Sand Road, five miles or so outside Columbus, Mississippi, among my friends was a weird kid who collected used condoms along one of the roads that led down to one of our swimming holes. The fundamentalists I grew up among didn't trust the pill, even when it became readily available, but everybody trusted the rubber, so there were plenty of them for him to collect. Billy (obviously not his real name) would collect the rubbers and little boxes and "coin packs" and take his treasure down to the Cold Hole and give the rubbers a good washing and hang them out to dry. After they were dry, he'd roll them back up and take them home to their barn and label the boxes with some girl's name. He probably used them on himself, but I never witnessed that. One day another boy and I discovered his trove and trashed it. I'll never forgot those little ghosts dangling among the rafters of the barn. He was mightily disturbed over our desecration and from that point on collected and washed and hid his little Caspers in a place we never found.

Tim Seibles, born in Philadelphia in 1955, is the author of several poetry collections including *Hurdy-Gurdy, Hammerlock,* and *Buffalo Head Solos.* His first book, *Body Moves,* (1988) has just been re-released by Carnegie Mellon U. Press as part of their Contemporary Classics series. His latest, *Fast Animal,* was a finalist for the 2012 National Book Award. In 2013 he received the Pen Oakland Josephine Miles Award for poetry and received an honorary Doctorate of Humane Letters from Misericordia University for his literary accomplishments. Most recently, he received the Theodore Roethke Memorial Poetry Award for *Fast Animal,* given triennially for a collection of poems. His poetry has been featured in several anthologies, including *Best American Poetry 2010* and *Best American Poetry 2013.* He has been a workshop leader for Cave Canem, a writer's retreat for African American poets, and lives in Norfolk, Virginia, where he is a member of the English and MFA in writing faculty at Old Dominion University.

About the '60s: By the late '60s, I was a young teenager in Philadelphia sporting a mid-size afro and watching what appeared to be several crucial movements happening simultaneously in our country. I was too young to be in the action, but I watched ravenously. There were the Black Panthers, the hippies, the civil rights activists, Gil Scott Heron telling me the revolution will not be televised, and, of course, the rise of hard rock—Jimi Hendrix was my main man on the music scene.

I was too young to grasp the full significance of what was happening, but old enough to know that something big was in motion. Although I was deeply in love with football at this point in my life—and wanted desperately to be a pro someday—the engagement with society's ills, the fierce artistic expression, and the resonance of the radical perspectives that defined the era left the deepest impressions on me.

Martha Serpas is the author of three collections of poetry, *Cote Blanche, The Dirty Side of the Storm,* and *The Diener.* Her work has appeared in *The New Yorker, The Nation, Image,* and *Southwest Review* as well as in the anthologies *American*

Religious Poems and *The Art of the Sonnet*. Active in efforts to restore Louisiana's wetlands, she co-produced *Veins in the Gulf*, a documentary about coastal erosion. She teaches in the Creative Writing Program at the University of Houston and also serves as a hospital trauma chaplain.

About the '60s: In the '60s on Bayou Lafourche, Louisiana, I was watching my sister grow up faster than me. My school had no air conditioning. (I had very frizzy hair.) I liked hurricanes because school was canceled, and I could walk around with a candle fixed to a mayonnaise lid. I also liked a really cold winter day because pipes froze and school was canceled. I didn't know it at the time, but feminism was building up strong. Had I known it would peak in the '70s, I would have paid more attention.

Alan Shapiro is author of 12 books of poetry (most recently *Reel to Reel*, finalist for the Pulitzer Prize, and *Night of the Republic*, a finalist for both the National Book Award and The Griffin Prize), 4 books of prose (including *Broadway Baby*, a novel from Algonquin Books). Winner of the, 2 NEAs, a Guggenheim and a Lila Wallace Reader's Digest Award, he is also winner of a Kingsley Tufts Award, *LA Times* Book Prize, and an award in literature from The American Academy of Arts and Letters of the American Academy of Arts and Sciences.

About the '60s: I was a teenager in the latter part of the 1960's. I have the dubious distinction of having gone to Woodstock, and the even more dubious distinction of being the only person there among the half a million people in attendance who was unable to procure either sex or drugs. I entered high school the same year busing started in Boston. I regard that piece of President Johnson's Great Society as one of the most formative experiences of my life. Busing gave me the opportunity to know intimately a whole group of people and a whole part of Boston I otherwise would not have known. I would not be the writer I am today had it not been for the spirit of the civil rights movement, the passing of which is the subject of my lament, "Between Assassinations."

Vivian Shipley, a CSU Distinguished Professor, teaches at Southern Connecticut State University. Two new books,

The Poet (Louisiana Literature Press at SLU) and *Perennial* (Negative Capability Press) were published in 2015. Her eighth book of poetry, *All of Your Messages Have Been Erased (2010, SLU)* was nominated for the Pulitzer Prize and won the 2011 Paterson Award for Sustained Literary Achievement, the Sheila Motton Book Award from New England Poetry Club and the CT Press Club Prize for Best Creative Writing. In 2010, her sixth chapbook, *Greatest Hits: 1974-2010* was published by Pudding House Press. Shipley has won 35 First Prize poetry awards for individual poems including the Lucille Medwick Prize from PSA, the Robert Frost Foundation Poetry Prize, Ann Stanford Poetry Prize from USC, the Marble Faun Poetry Prize from Pirate's Alley William Faulkner Society, the Daniel Varoujan Prize from NEPC, and the Hart Crane Prize from Kent State.

About the '60s: In the '60s, my life was traditional. A 1960 high school graduate, I didn't consider going out of state and went to University of Kentucky. Graduating in 1964, I married in 1965, moved to New Haven, CT with my husband, a Yale medical student, and taught 3 years at Guilford Junior High. In 1968, I entered Vanderbilt's PhD program because my husband interned there; he returned to Yale after one year. In September, 1969, I applied to be an adjunct at Southern Connecticut State University and was offered a tenure track position instead. I'm still there. The '70s when I wrote these poems were a different story.

Patricia Smith is the author of seven critically acclaimed books of poetry, including *Gotta Go Gotta Flow,* a collaboration with award-winning Chicago photographer Michael Abramson; *Shoulda Been Jimi Savannah,* which received the 2014 Rebekah Bobbitt Prize from the Library of Congress and the 2013 Lenore Marshall Poetry Prize; *Blood Dazzler,* a National Book Award finalist; and *Teahouse of the Almighty,* a National Poetry Series winner. Other collections of poetry include *Close to Death; Big Towns, Big Talk;* and *Life According to Motown.* She also edited an edition of a crime fiction anthology, *Staten Island Noir,* and wrote the children's book, *Janna and the Kings.* Recipient of fellowships to Yaddo and the McDowell Colony, she is recognized as one of the world's most formidable performers.

About the '60s: I was 10 years old in 1965, totally under the sway of a church-obsessed mother. She and my father—the center of my universe—had just split, my father had moved out of the house, and my hair began falling out. In 1968, after the assassination of Matin Luther King, our entire neighborhood burned to a smoldering rubble. The West Side—the part of town everyone told everyone to say away from—was the place in Chicago that housed most of those hopeful fugitives from the South. After the riots, it became even more isolated. In 1968, the year I discovered hippies, SDS and the thought of drugs, was also the year I was gainly, awkward and unable to do a damn thing to make a difference. Or so I thought. I had a pen.

Katherine Solomon's poems have appeared in journals such as *Green Mountains Review*, *The Worcester Review*, *Naugatuck River Review, and Solidus,* among others, and in anthologies *including Orpheus & Company: Contemporary Poems on Greek Mythology*, & *The 2008 Poets' Guide to New Hampshire.* Her chapbook, *Tempting Fate*, is available from Oyster River Press. A second chapbook, *Transit of Venus*, was published by Finishing Line Press in 2015.

About the '60s: My roommate and I moved from Cambridge, MA to Toronto, when her boyfriend, a renegade chemist known to drug agents in the US, Canada, and Great Britain as "Dr. Speedo," or "The Wizard," had to flee the country. He supplemented his legal income by making crystal meth, but his passion was for formulating exotic psychedelics like DMT and MDA, that were not yet illegal. We had the good fortune to be his "research assistants" for several years. The events in "Expatriates: 1967" occurred shortly after we arrived in Toronto. "A Momentarily Subdued Foofaraw" describes a subsequent DMT afternoon in Florida. I met my husband on a commune in 1970. We have lived in Sutton, NH for thirty-six years, raising two children and many organic vegetables.

Leon Stokesbury has lived his life in the South, first in Texas and Arkansas and Louisiana, then, for the past 25 years, as a teacher in the graduate writing program at Georgia State University in Atlanta. His first book, *Often in Different Landscapes*, was a co-winner of the first AWP Poetry Competition in 1975. He also edited several anthologies, including *The Made Thing: An Anthology of Contemporary Southern Poetry*, and *Articles of War: American Poetry about World War II*. His *Autumn Rhythm: New & Selected Poems* won The Poets' Prize in 1998, and, more recently, his poem, "Watching My Mother Take Her Last Breath," was awarded a Pushcart Prize in 2013.

About the '60s: Back in those wonderful years, when it never occurred to any of us that we would ever die, I lived in the pine forests six or seven miles outside a little town called Silsbee, Texas. It seems now that that whole region of East Texas was still in the '50s. Then came 1968, and I went off to graduate school at the University of Arkansas. Culture shock. Beautiful chaos and art and poetry and assorted experiments and freedom and lovely women. All at once. The rest is history.

Lorenzo Thomas was a professor of English at the University of Houston for over two decades. He made important contributions to the study of African-American Literature. In 2000, he published *Extraordinary Measures: Afrocentric Modernism and 20th-Century American Poetry*, his overview of the work of James Fenton and Amiri Baraka, among others. His other books are *Chances are Few, The Bathers, Dancing on Main Street*, and *Don't Deny My Name*, (edited and with an introduction by Aldon Lynn Nielsen). Thomas had a large influence on Houston culture in literature and music; he was instrumental in organizing Juneteenth Blues Festivals in Houston and other Texas cities. Thomas was one of the lynch-pins that held together the disparate small presses of Texas throughout the '70s.

About the '60s: Lorenzo Thomas was a graduate of Queens College in New York. During his years there, he joined the Umbra Workshops, which served as a crucible for emerging black poets. The workshop was one of the currents that fed the black arts movement of the '60s and '70s, the first major African-American artistic movement after the Harlem Renaissance. After graduating college, Thomas joined the Navy and served as an advisor in Vietnam in 1971. Born in 1944, he died in 2005.

Natasha Trethewey served two terms as the 19th Poet Laureate of the United States (2012-2014). She is the author of four collections of poetry: *Domestic Work, Bellocq's Ophelia* (Graywolf, 2002); *Native Guard* (Houghton Mifflin, 2006), for which she was awarded the 2007 Pulitzer Prize; and *Thrall* (Houghton Mifflin Harcourt, August 2012.) She is also the author of *Beyond Katrina: A Meditation on the Mississippi Gulf Coast* (University of Georgia Press, 2010). Recipient of fellowships from the NEA and the Guggenheim and Rockefeller Foundations among other honors, her work has appeared in several volumes of *Best American Poetry*. At Emory University she is Robert W. Woodruff Professor of English and Creative Writing.

About the '60s: I was born in Mississippi in 1966. There, and in as many as twenty states in the nation, my parents' interracial marriage was illegal. They had married in 1965 in Ohio. In 1967, with the Loving v. State of Virginia decision, the Supreme Court ruled that anti-miscegenation laws were unconstitutional.

Diane Wakoski, born in Southern California, educated at UC, Berkeley, made her home and began her poetry career in New York City 1960-1973. She earned her living as a book store clerk, a junior high school teacher in Manhattan and, for ten years on-the-road, giving poetry readings on college campuses. From 1975, she was Poet In Residence and University Distinguished Professor at Michigan State University, retiring in 2012. Since her first chapbook, *Coins and Coffins*, (Hawk's Well Press1962) she has been published in more than 25 collections of poetry, one of which, *Emerald Ice: Selected Poems 1962-1987*, won the William Carlos Williams prize from the Poetry Society of America. Since 2000, when her last collection to be published by Black Sparrow Press, *The Butcher's Apron*, appeared, she has completed two collections, *The Diamond Dog* and *Bay of Angels*, (Anhinga Press, 2010 and 2013). One of the poems in *Bay of Angels* was selected for a Pushcart Prize and published in their anthology *Pushcart Prize XXXVII: Best of the Small Presses*, 2013.

About the '60s: I was excited, as if shocked by electricity, writing poems as fast as I thought of them, and desperate for people to hear me, to listen to my voice. In the early '60s I was living in New York, first with avant garde composer, La Monte Young and then for a brief time with Minimalist artist, Robert Morris. Consequently, I met composers, musicians, artists and dancers, and found myself absorbing wild, new aesthetics and ideas of art. Simultaneously I was religiously attending twice a week the Lower East-Side poetry readings that evolved through the '60s, from the Tenth St. Coffee House, to the Second Avenue Coffee House, then followed by the Deux Megots Cafe, and finally the St. Mark's Poetry Project. These weekly opportunities to read my poetry at the open mikes helped to give me confidence and a sense that I was heard and appreciated, as I wanted to be. Though I always had a 9-6 day-job to pay the rent, I spent all of my cognizant time writing poetry or being at readings. I had no social life.

Michael Waters' books include *Celestial Joyride* (2016), *Gospel Night* (2011), *Darling Vulgarity* (2006—finalist for the *Los Angeles Times* Book Prize), & *Parthenopi: New and Selected Poems* (2001—finalist for the Paterson Poetry Prize) from BOA Editions. He has co-edited *Contemporary American Poetry* (Houghton Mifflin, 2006) & *Perfect in Their Art: Poems on Boxing from Homer to Ali* (Southern Illinois UP, 2003). The recipient of five Pushcart Prizes & fellowships from the NEA, Fulbright Foundation & NJ State Council on the Arts, Waters teaches at Monmouth University & in the Drew University MFA Program in Poetry and Poetry in Translation.

About the '60s: "Sixties Sonnet." In 1969 I attended the Woodstock festival, start to finish, with my lovely girlfriend Denise, losing my summer job as camp counselor by not returning to work on time on Monday morning. I had been warned, but I understood even then that seeing Jimi Hendrix perform "The Star Spangled Banner" in those early hours was more important than my final two weeks' salary. As was spooning in the back seat of the Chevy Nova convertible when exhaustion drew us into an A&P parking lot on the ride home.

"Dog in Space." The Russians first sent a dog ("Laika") into space in 1957. Others followed in 1960, 1961, and 1966. The songs mentioned in the poem topped the charts in 1963 and 1960, respectively. Little Peggy March chirped "I Will Follow Him." Elvis Presley crooned "It's Now or Never." I ask rock 'n' roll purists to forgive me for fudging the chronology.

"Christ at the Apollo, 1962." James Brown's seminal LP, *Live at the Apollo*, was recorded on October 24, 1962, and released in 1963. The epigraph by Whitman is taken from his essay "Democratic Vistas" (1871); the poem was triggered, in part, by a conversation with novelist Richard Price who had once interviewed James Brown. At Price's request, the Godfather of Soul had hoisted his trousers to display his knees, damaged by years of dropping to the stage at the climax of his show.

Randall Watson's *The Sleep Accusations* received the Blue Lynx Poetry Award at Eastern Washington University, and is currently available through Carnegie Mellon University Press. His first book, *Las Delaciones del Sueno*, was published in a bi-lingual edition by the Universidad Veracruzana in Xalapa, Mexico. His novella, *Petals*, (under the pseudonym Ellis Reece) won the *Quarterly West* Novella Competition. He is also the editor of *The Weight of Addition* (Mutabilis Press), an anthology of Texas poetry.

About the '60s: I was a child, west of the Hardy Boys, north of the Great South Bay, drawing weakfish from the waters. Then as my body grew, I moved, all too quickly, towards Tompkins Square and Delancey, watching my ignorance skitter like an old deck-shoe heaved by the seawash back to the world's fullness. Even now I'm barely speakable, so filled I was by its beauty, its suchness, its hedonism and disgust.

Scott Wiggerman is the author of two poetry books, *Presence* (Pecan Grove, 2011) and *Vegetables and Other Relationships* (Plain View, 2000), and the editor of several volumes, including the best-selling *Wingbeats: Exercises & Practice in Poetry* (2011), *Lifting the Sky: Southwestern Haiku & Haiga* (2013), and *Wingbeats II* (2014). With three Pushcart nominations, he is a frequent workshop instructor and chief editor for Dos Gatos Press in Austin, Texas, publisher of the annual *Texas Poetry Calendar*. Recent publications include *Wilde Magazine, Floating Bridge Review, Decades Review, Frogpond, Pinyon Review, Borderlands: Texas Poetry Review*, and the anthologies *This Assignment Is So Gay* and *Forgetting Home: Poems about Alzheimer's*.

About the '60s: In the '60s, I graduated from grade school to high school, living in suburban Chicago, where I was heavily influenced by the brouhaha of the 1968 Democratic Convention, and its clashes between the Establishment and the Yuppies. The Beatles, the Airplane, and the radicalized environment of Chicago turned me liberal at an early age, and I've never turned back. "Before the Pill" is a critique of the idealized housewife of '60s' television versus the reality of my own mother and "her kind," to quote Sexton.

Richard Wilbur's many honors include the National Book Award and two Pulitzer Prizes for his poetry. His translations of French verse are highly praised by critics; his *Tartuffe* by Moliere won the Bollingen Prize. Wilbur was the 2nd Poet Laureate of the United States. After teaching for a time at Smith and at his alma mater, Amherst, he retired to Cummington, Massachusetts, where, he says, "I see more cows than people."

    About the '60s: "Student Strikers," as it suggests, was written at a time when many students were protesting our country's military adventures.

C. K. Williams' most recent book of prose poetry, *All at Once*, was published in 2014. His previous book, *Writers Writing Dying*, came out in 2012. His latest books of criticism are *In Time: Poems, Poets, and the Rest* and a study of Walt Whitman, *On Whitman*. He has published translations of Sophocles' *Women of Trachis*, Euripides' Bacchae, and books of poems by Francis Ponge and Adam Zagajewski. Williams has won the Pulitzer Prize, the National Book Award, and the National Book Critics Circle Award, among many others, and has taught at several universities, including NYU, Columbia, and George Mason University. He retired in 2013 from the Creative Writing Program at Princeton University. He is a member of the American Academy of Arts and Letters.

    About the '60s: What I remember most and with the greatest pleasure about the '60s is the way the decade was so much an educational experience, in poetry, in art, in politics, in life. Everything was changing—the possibilities of poetry, the opportunities of new ways of perceiving the world and thinking about it—and while all this was fulfilling it was also demanding. Something always seemed to be being asked of you, of your ethical standards, of your aesthetic assumptions. All this is true of course of any moment in history, but during those ten or so years it all seemed accelerated, compressed, everything under pressure. It wasn't always easy, but it was thrilling, to have lived it, and to remember.

Kathleen Winter is the author of *Nostalgia for the Criminal Past* (Elixir Press, 2012), which won the 2012 Antivenom Poetry Prize and the 2013 Texas Institute of Letters Bob Bush Memorial Award. She has received fellowships from James Merrill House Foundation; Brown Foundation Residency at the Dora Maar House, Ménerbes, France; Vermont Studio Center; Virginia G. Piper Center; and the Prague Summer Program. She holds an M.F.A. from Arizona State University; J.D. from University of California, Davis; M.A. from Boston College; and B.A. from the University of Texas at Austin. Her poems have appeared in *Tin House, Poetry London, AGNI, Field, The New Republic, The Cincinnati Review, Gulf Coast* and other journals. Winter teaches writing and literature at Napa Valley College and serves as an assistant editor for *Volt*.

About the '60s: During the '60s I was a rather small child living in San Antonio, Texas. I remember grainy television coverage of the moon landing, and much public and familial zeal regarding the space program. The poem "Nostalgia for Apollo" was sparked decades later by watching "In the Shadow of the Moon," David Sington's fine documentary about the Apollo missions.

Paula Anne Yup has over one hundred published poems, including those appearing in *The Third Woman: Minority Women Writers of the United States, Passages North Anthology, What Book!?, Mid-American Review, J Journal*, and several Outrider Press anthologies. Her first book of poetry, *Making a Clean Space in the Sky*, was recently published by Evening Street Press. She was born in Phoenix, Arizona, and received her M.F.A. from Vermont College. After living in the Marshall Islands for a dozen years, she moved to Spokane, Washington.

About the '60s: During the '60s I attended Madrid School in Phoenix and worked at B & E with my parents and siblings. The customers rioted and soon after, the store bit the dust. I remember that customers broke the windows. My terrified parents locked the doors. After that my mother got cashiering jobs in supermarkets. "Waiting" was written after a phone conversation I had with my sister and is based on a memory of my sister's. I remember first grade as a time of tears. I learned to read with Dr. Seuss books. My first sorrow was JFK's assassination. As a first grader, I remember my teacher bursting into tears.

Acknowledgments

Note: Different authors preferred different forms of citation, so the editors opted, appropriately for this volume, for diversity of form over regularity.

Ai, "Cuba, 1962." Copyright © 1973 by Ai, from *Vice: New and Selected Poems by Ai*. Used by permission of W. W. Norton & Company, Inc.

Robert Alexander, "A Joe Pass Guitar Solo" reprinted by permission of author.

Michael Anania, "A Second-Hand Elegy" reprinted by permission of the author.

Judith Arcana, "Correspondence," "The Sun in Montana," and "Women's Liberation" reprinted by permission of the author.

Peter Balakian, "Reading Dickinson/Summer '68" from *Ziggurat* (University of Chicago Press, 2010), reprinted by permission of the author.

Rebecca Balcárcel, "*Ave* America" first appeared in *North American Review,* reprinted by permission of author.

Wendy Barker, "*The Feminine Mystique,*" "Teaching *Uncle Tom's Children,*" and "Miniskirts," from *Nothing Between Us* (Del Sol Press, 2009), reprinted by permission of the author.

Aliki Barnstone, "In the Workshop" first appeared in *Crab Orchard Review*. Reprinted by permission of the author.

Chana Bloch, "Chez Pierre, 1961" originally appeared in *Poetry;* reprinted in *The Past Keeps Changing* (Sheep Meadow, 1992). "The Spoils" originally appeared in *Tikkun;* reprinted in *Blood Honey* (Autumn House, 2009). Both poems reprinted here from *Swimming in the Rain: New & Selected Poems, 1980-2015* (Autumn House, 2015) by permission of the author.

Robert Bly, "At a March Against the Vietnam War: Washington, November 27, 1965," "Driving West in 1970"

Fleda Brown, "Tillywilly Fog" from *The Women Who Loved Elvis All Their Lives* (Carnegie Mellon University Press, 2004). Reprinted by permission of the author.

W. E. Butts, "The Industrial Diamonds of 1964" "The Other Language" and "Our Fathers' Clothes" reprinted by permission of S. Stephanie for W. E. Butts.

Ana Castillo, "Dirty Mexican" appeared in *My Father Was a Toltec and Selected Poems* (New York: Norton, 1995). Used by permission of the author and W.W. Norton & Company, Inc.

Lorna Dee Cervantes, "Cream" appeared in *Drive: The First Quartet* (Wings Press, 2006), reprinted by permission of the author.

Kevin Clark, "Eight Hours in the Nixon Era" was first published in *Notre Dame Review*, reprinted in *Self-Portrait With Expletives* (Pleides Press, 2010), reprinted here by permission of the author.

Ginny Lowe Connors, "Optical Longings and Illusions" was first published in *The Unparalleled Beauty of a Crooked Line* (Antrim House Books, 2012).

Jim Daniels, "Jimi Hendrix, National Anthem," "Soul Sacrifice," and "Shedding the Sixties," reprinted by permission of the author.

Kate Daniels, "War Photograph" from *Niobe Poems*, © 1988, reprinted by permission of the University of Pittsburgh Press. "Late Apology to Doris Haskins" and "Homage to Calvin Spotswood" from *A Walk In Victoria's Secret* (2010), reprinted by permission of Louisiana State University Press.

Lucille Lang Day, "Fifteen" was first published in *The Hudson Review* and reprinted in *Wild One (2000)*, reprinted here by permission of the author. "Reject Jell-O" was first published in *The Hudson Review* and reprinted in *Wild One* (2000) as well as read by Garrison Keillor on *The Writer's Almanac*, July 25, 2005, reprinted here by permission of the author. "The Trip" from *Wild One* (2000), reprinted by permission of the author.

Toi Derricotte, "Blackbottom," from *Captivity* (1990), University of Pittsburgh Press, reprinted by permission of the author.

Wings Press was founded in 1975 by Joanie Whitebird and Joseph F. Lomax, both deceased, as "an informal association of artists and cultural mythologists dedicated to the preservation of the literature of the nation of Texas." Publisher, editor and designer since 1995, Bryce Milligan is honored to carry on and expand that mission to include the finest in American writing— meaning all of the Americas, without commercial considerations clouding the decision to publish or not to publish.

Wings Press intends to produce multicultural books, chapbooks, ebooks, recordings and broadsides that enlighten the human spirit and enliven the mind. Everyone ever associated with Wings has been or is a writer, and we believe that writing is a transformational art form capable of changing the world, primarily by allowing us to glimpse something of each other's souls. We believe that good writing is innovative, insightful, and interesting. But most of all it is honest. As Bob Dylan put it, "To live outside the law, you must be honest."

Likewise, Wings Press is committed to treating the planet itself as a partner. Thus the press uses as much recycled material as possible, from the paper on which the books are printed to the boxes in which they are shipped.

As Robert Dana wrote in *Against the Grain*, "Small press publishing is personal publishing. In essence, it's a matter of personal vision, personal taste and courage, and personal friendships." Welcome to our world.

COLOPHON

This first edition of *Far Out: Poems of the '60s*, edited by Wendy Barker and Dave Parsons, has been printed on 55 pound Edwards Brothers "natural" paper containing a percentage of recycled fiber. Titles have been set in Psychedelic Smoke, Whiffy and Papyrus type, the text in Adobe Caslon type. This book was designed by Bryce Milligan.

On-line catalogue and ordering:
www.wingspress.com
Wings Press titles are distributed to the trade by the
Independent Publishers Group
www.ipgbook.com
and in Europe by Gazelle
www.gazellebookservices.co.uk

Also available as an ebook.